LITURGICAL
SENSE

WEIL SERIES IN LITURGICS

LITURGICAL SENSE

The Logic of Rite

LOUIS WEIL

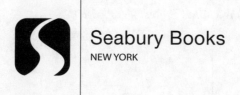

Seabury Books
NEW YORK

Unless otherwise noted, the Scripture quotations contained
herein are from the New Revised Standard Version Bible,
copyright © 1989 by the Division of Christian Education of
the National Council of Churches of Christ in the U.S.A.
Used by permission. All rights reserved.

Cover design by Laurie Klein Westhafer
Typeset by Denise Hoff

Library of Congress Cataloging-in-Publication Data

Weil, Louis, 1935–
    Liturgical sense: the logic of rite / Louis Weil.
        pages cm
    Includes bibliographical references.
    ISBN 978-1-59627-243-9 (pbk.)
    ISBN 978-1-59627-244-6 (ebook) 1. Liturgics. 2. Episcopal
Church. Book of common prayer (1979) I. Title.
    BV176.3.W45 2013
    264'.03--dc23
                        2012047298

Seabury Books
445 Fifth Avenue
New York, New York 10016

www.churchpublishing.org
An imprint of Church Publishing Incorporated

Printed in the United States of America

Contents

Introduction
to the Series

LOUIS WEIL'S ACADEMIC LIFE HAS paralleled the liturgical renewal that led up to—and grew out of—Vatican II. It has been a rich time of liturgical scholarship from the new discoveries regarding the Apostolic era to the latest research in neuropsychology and ritual studies. Louis Weil has been a pioneer in the scholarship of a generation.

In a teaching ministry of over fifty years, Weil

has taught liturgical and sacramental studies at three Episcopal seminaries, in Puerto Rico, in Wisconsin, and in California. He has given programs for laity and clergy on five continents, and has written, either in books or articles, about the major aspects of liturgical renewal in the United States and abroad. In 2012, the North American Academy of Liturgy presented him with its *Berakah Award* for his work as a teacher of liturgy both ecumenically and in the Anglican Communion.

It is in recognition of his work in and on behalf of the Church he so loves that Church Publishing is proud to introduce the Weil Series in Liturgics, an occasional series dedicated to the sort of liturgical and academic scholarship that has been the hallmark of Weil's professional life.

Nancy Bryan
Editorial Director for Books and Music
Church Publishing, Inc.

A Note
Concerning the Title

THE WORD 'SENSE' IN THE title of this book is intended to connect with two aspects of liturgical practice. It refers to the meaning of a rite or a part of a rite with regard to its historical and theological development in Christian liturgical evolution. In other words, how did a particular rite originate and develop within a specific liturgical context and tradition? Thus, what is the 'sense' of the rite?

But there is also a second way that 'sense' is

being used. This use of the word emerges from the fact that a liturgical practice may be *meaningful* to the person who does it, but may be quite obscure or even confusing to the congregation who observes it. In this latter context, such practices can be quite erosive of the general liturgical understanding of "the common sense" of the rite. This situation can produce liturgical practices that are quite extraneous to the inherent meaning of the rite itself.

The primary focus of this book is the first meaning—theological and liturgical sensibility—but we shall also consider examples of the second meaning which have emerged in recent practice.

Preface

DURING THE YEARS SINCE 1979, when the new American *Book of Common Prayer* received its final authorization at the General Convention, a large number of liturgical manuals have been published. These various manuals have reflected a wide range of ritual practices that may be used by presiders and other ministers in the celebration of the prayer book rites. These publications vary from quite simple models to adaptations of the elaborate models which were a distinctive mark of Anglo-Catholic practice and which were generally based on Roman Catholic models from the time prior to the Second Vatican Council.

This book is not being offered as yet another addition to the already substantial number of such manuals. What I have set out to do here is explore the underlying level of all such ritual prac- tices: How have any such rituals developed in the Church over the centuries? What are the historical and cultural as well as theological factors that have shaped these diverse models? Why have our litur- gical leaders, mostly ordained bishops and priests, favored certain practices and continued to do them even when their meaning has become obscured by the passage of time?

This last question points to a very common problem in the formation of those who are to be ordained, as well as for people who have served for years in the ordained ministries. I have noticed many times that clergy have opted for a specific model of liturgical ministry quite early, perhaps even before ordination, and that once this model is established, later critical reflection upon it seldom takes place. It is very easy to become set into a ritual pattern and never to engage it subsequently, but simply to continue practicing it, as it were, by rote. When I have raised a question about a ritual practice with clergy, the answer too often has been, "But I have always done it that way."

Due to the timing of my own doctoral study of

the liturgy, coming as it did during the liturgical revolution precipitated for Roman Catholics by the Second Vatican Council, as well as during the years leading up to the revision and authorization of a new American *Book of Common Prayer* in 1979, I was obliged to reconsider the liturgical model that I had adopted at the time of my ordination to the priesthood. In retrospect, I feel that this was providential, and it gave me a perspective that has contributed profoundly to my work as a teacher and specifically in the preparation of candidates for ordination in the Episcopal Church. But at the time that I was first confronted with the need to abandon aspects of my Anglo-Catholic model because of a deepening insight into the place of liturgical ministry in the life of the Church, it was a wrenching experience. My model of presiding at the Eucharist had taken an important place in my spirituality as a priest. This change in my own experience is a major motivation for this book, to help readers understand the theological and historical reasons for this change in our general sense of the role of the presider at the liturgy.

I want to express my gratitude to those who have contributed in special ways to the development of this book: first, to a very large multitude, and second, to one person.

First, to the students whom I have taught in a ministry of over a half-century: your questions and responses both in class and beyond have challenged me to think ever more deeply on these questions than I could have done without such prodding.

Second, I am deeply grateful to my editor Nancy Bryan, first, for asking me to write this book, but then for staying with me as it has developed. Her attentive eye has helped me to sharpen my focus on the primary issue: how does the ministry of a presider at the liturgy encourage or inhibit the full participation of God's people who have gathered for the rites of Christian faith. Her insight has been a tremendous gift.

Louis Weil

CHAPTER 1

Why a Concern about Ritual?

THE ORIGINS OF THIS BOOK lie in my experience with students during a half-century as a teacher of liturgy. As my style of teaching developed, I found it quite natural to draw upon my experience as a worshiper and as a person who has participated in liturgical celebrations in a wide variety of contexts. In that experience I have quite often simply been an ordinary Christian in a pew on Sunday morning, but always with my eyes wide open as to what I was seeing and hearing in that particular celebration.

I have learned that it makes an enormous

difference if a priest is the presider, or an assisting minister, every Sunday. The perspective shaped in that context can inhibit an awareness of the view from the congregation. Generally speaking, clergy may be expected to know what is intended in the rite, but what is it that the people *see*? As we shall observe in this book, what the people see is sometimes quite different from what is intended.

In the context of the classroom and in my work with seminarians, I have always been aware that the students were candidates for ordination for whom a course in liturgical studies must include an orientation toward their own future ministries. After ordination they would have pastoral responsibility for the liturgical norms of the community to which their bishop would assign them. It was in this context that I came regularly to draw upon my own experiences as a worshiper, and to point out both the positive and the negative aspects of countless liturgies in which I had participated over the years.

Thus, in my teaching I chose not to speak only at a theoretical level in which a teacher might be concerned primarily with reference to historical or theological data. As appropriate, I aimed at placing the wide range of liturgical issues within the context of actual liturgical experience. Sometimes these were quite positive examples of what one might describe as good liturgical models upon which a pastoral norm might be based. Similarly, when I described a poor liturgical model, I was able to analyze with the students why this model was not effective, or even how it embodied a theological understanding which actually contradicted the theology of the Church as to the meaning of the rite. This method brought home to them an awareness that the parish priest is not merely repeating the authorized words found in the *Book of Common Prayer*, but is also, in the ritual choices that are made, embodying the theology in which the rites were grounded—or potentially, even if unintentionally, subverting that theology.

This approach was nurtured in me through the experience of my own seminary formation with regard both to the theology of the sacraments and the understanding of liturgical worship which is the foundation of the prayer book tradition in Anglicanism. At the time of my own seminary training, these two aspects of the liturgy were actually taught in two different contexts. The attention given to sacramental theology played a relatively minor role in the basic course in theology.

What is most striking to me in this is that when, for example, Baptism was discussed in class, no reference whatever was made to the rite of Baptism as found in the then-authorized American *Book of Common Prayer* of 1928. Similarly, the Eucharist was discussed, again not in great depth, without reference to the text of *The Order for Holy Communion* as it was being celebrated throughout the Episcopal Church, including our seminary community each morning in the chapel.

I have asked myself countless times why sacramental theology was given little attention, and why what was taught did not make reference to how a sacrament was celebrated in the prayer book rites. I think that at least part of the answer is that there was a general feeling that, after all, "we know what Baptism is; we all know what Eucharist is . . . and we know what Ordination is." But the extraordinary flowering of research on the sacraments during the past few decades has shown us that both historically and theologically we had only an impoverished sense of the rich complexity of these rites and their meaning in the history of Christianity.

When I look back on the approach to the teaching of liturgy that was standard during my seminary years through the lens of my personal experience as a teacher of liturgy, I find it quite amazing that the two primary sacramental actions of the Church were not discussed with any reference to how the Church actually embodied the theology of these two "dominical sacraments" in our liturgical celebrations. There was a kind of disconnection, which of course I accepted at the time as a seminarian, but which I came to reject in my own ministry as a teacher. Years later, in conversations with clergy who had attended seminaries other than my own, I learned that the approach I had experienced was characteristic of the general approach to the teaching of liturgy across the Episcopal Church at that time.

Although the curriculum at my seminary did include a required course which was titled "Liturgics," many other schools did not require even a basic course in liturgical studies. When I inquired about this, I was told that in some places liturgy was seen as a matter of "practical theology"—thus not an academic subject with which the seminary faculty should be concerned. It was expected that a newly ordained deacon would learn these practical aspects of ordained ministry during the one-year curacy that was then normative upon completion of the three-year seminary program.

Other aspects of liturgical study, such as the historical evolution of the liturgy in the life of the Church, including the developments and conflicts about its theological meanings, might be available as electives for seminarians for whom this was an area of special interest. But when it came to what a presider or officiant might actually *do* in matters of ritual practice, most of the newly ordained would be shaped by the particular manner and style of the rector at the parish where they were assigned, from whom they would learn how the rites were to be done—at least in that particular parish. To be frank, often the rector's own seminary training in liturgy had left him, in this regard, with little more than his own preferences.

Among Anglicans, the primary intention was always a kind of liturgical obedience to the particular rite, not only the authorized words of the rite, but also the rubrics within the rite. Although those rubrics tended to be rather minimal in the various versions of the *Book of Common Prayer* as authorized in the provinces of the Anglican Communion, they were considered as obligatory as the texts themselves as an expression of prayer book conformity which a candidate promised at the time of ordination. For clergy formed in this tradition, fidelity to the rubrics was seen as their primary obligation with regard to the performance of the rites of the *Book of Common Prayer*. This absolute conformity was generally obeyed in principle more than in practice, since, as I observed again and again in visits to different parishes, adherence to the *Book of Common Prayer* was interpreted to mean an adherence to the local model, that is, to "the Prayer Book as we do it here." But the principle of prayer book conformity itself operated as a powerful symbol of Anglican unity.[1]

---

1. See my essay, "The Holy Spirit: Source of Unity in the Liturgy," in *Anglican Theological Review* 83 (3), Summer 2001, 409–15. Republished in Robert B. Slocum, ed., *Engaging the Spirit: Essays on the Life and Theology of the Holy Spirit* (New York: Church Publishing, 2001), 39–45.

In conversations with Roman Catholic priests
of my generation, I discovered that their liturgical
formation had as its focus the learning of the canon
law concerned with the liturgy, as well as the authorized rubrics for each sacramental act that a priest
was to perform. The goal of this focus on liturgical
law and rubrics was intended to give the assurance
to the priest (and to his bishop!) that he was con-
forming to the intention of the Church in sacramental celebrations so that validity was assured.
With regard to the celebration of the Mass, the
rubrics had developed as an elaborate and precise
pattern, which was an integral requirement for the
priest in his task to fulfill that intention.

For many of the ordained, this understanding
of their ritual obligations had significant impact
upon their whole approach to the liturgical rites.
The effect of this for both Anglicans and Roman
Catholics, although for different reasons, was to
limit liturgical practice to a very narrow range of
the practices of the Church as embodied at various
times and in various contexts. In other words, liturgical practice—the ritual models that have been
used by ordained pastoral leaders over the centuries—has been very diverse. Knowledge of this is
one of the liberating effects of the historical study
of the liturgy. One learns through such study that
everything in the liturgy carries a history, an evolution that has been shaped through a wide range

of factors, not merely theological, but also historical and cultural, and even through the accidents
of history.

In this book we shall explore a series of subjects
related to the general area of ritual eucharistic
practice. This will permit us to observe how the
"rubrical mentality" developed most significantly
as the Church shifted in its understanding of ordination from a model of service to the people of God,
to a model of sacramental power which was limited
to the ministries of bishops and priests. This shift
tended to isolate the ordained priest from the lives
of the people alongside whom, in the earlier model,
the sacramental rites had embodied and nourished
their shared life of faith.

We shall be examining in this book how the role
of a priest, primarily in the context of a eucharistic celebration, developed in ever more elaborate and dominant ways so that this great common
act of faith of the whole people of God became,
in effect, the private devotion of the priest which
the lay people might be permitted to observe but
in which they had no integral role.[2] Then we shall
see how the issues related to the sacramental role
of a priest were transformed in the sixteenth-cen-
tury English Reformation and were subsequently

2. Cf. Cyrille Vogel, "From the Eucharist to the Private Mass," in
Herman Schmidt, S.J., ed., *Liturgy: Self-Expression of the Church*
(Concilium 72; New York: Herder and Herder, 1972), 14–18.

modified through a new advent of ritualism in the nineteenth-century. Finally we shall consider how these questions are being approached with a new orientation in our own time as the Church rediscovers the authentic nature of liturgical prayer.

CHAPTER 2

A Different Ritual Room

W ITH THE COMPLETION OF THE process by which the Episcopal Church prepared its new edition of the *Book of Common Prayer*,[1] and at the time of its final authorization at the General Convention of 1979, the pastoral need for another, complementary, type of liturgical book arose. This second type of liturgical book would not have the same official status that is accorded by Anglicans to their respective versions

---

1. *The Book of Common Prayer and Administration of the Sacraments and Other Rites and Ceremonies of the Church* (New York: The Church Hymnal Corp., 1979).

of the *Book of Common Prayer* in the provinces of the Communion around the world. Even within the Episcopal Church, this second type of book would appear in many different versions, versions reflecting the wide range of ritual customs that are characteristic of Anglican liturgical practice. This second type would deal with questions about how the newly authorized book was to be used, how the various rites were to become embodied in local liturgical practice.

Ritual guides became a familiar complement to liturgical practice in the English Church from the seventeenth century in particular. By and large, these books were a defense of Anglican liturgical practice in response to the heated criticisms of the Puritans with regard to any use of fixed forms in worship. Such liturgical guides did not have the official or legal status of the authorized use of the *Book of Common Prayer*, but they were widely influential in establishing normative models in Anglican liturgical practice.

There were and are, of course, many clergy who never consult this type of book. They presume that the prayer book itself will contain a sufficient indication of how the rites are to be done, as expressed in the *rubrics* found in each rite.[2] But for a great

---

2. The word "rubric" is derived from the Latin *rubrica*, which referred to the use of the color red, such as red chalk. From the thirteenth century, the word appeared as a reference to a highlighted letter, word, or heading. This practice was taken over into liturgical manuscripts to indicate actions which the priest was to do. This stood in contrast to words that were to be spoken, that is, the actual texts, which were printed in black.

many clergy as well as for laity who are interested in the Church's worship and who perhaps are involved in liturgical planning, such books can serve as an important resource. These books offer what might be called a further development of the rubrics printed within the rites. They are a kind of expansion of the rubrics and are expressive of the particular liturgical preferences or style of their author. In some cases, a book may suggest quite minimal gestures with regard to how a rite is to be celebrated. In other examples, the ritual style that is modeled can be a very elaborate expansion of the rubrics, which are themselves characteristically brief. The rubrics generally do not spell out ritual choices in detail if for no other reason than the buildings in which the rites will be celebrated vary enormously in design, often imposing serious restraints upon how a rite will be performed.

Another characteristic of ritual manuals is that they will often simply reaffirm ritual models that were commonly used in connection with an earlier version of the prayer book, or only with very slight variations or modifications. For ordained clergy, this would probably be the most natural pattern to follow. When priests have celebrated a rite for many years using a particular pattern of ritual gestures, it is easy to presume that these gestures will continue in use. That pattern, whether simple or elaborate, has, through repeated use over many years, become their natural "body language" as liturgical presiders. The only modifications may be in connection with the spoken texts, which are now authorized in the new book.

In other cases, however, one may find a new approach as to how the ritual questions are to be engaged. This has been particularly true with regard to the American BCP of 1979. The reason for this change is that the people who drafted the new rites were doing more than a minimal revision of the earlier 1928 *Book of Common Prayer*. During the previous several decades, the impact of what is called "the Liturgical Movement" had begun to have a significant influence upon how liturgical ritual itself was to be understood.

Whereas earlier versions of the prayer book had embodied a liturgical model in which the ordained priest was the major and dominant agent in the liturgical action, the Liturgical Movement had awakened Christians in all of the liturgical churches to the root meaning of the word "liturgy"—that the liturgy is the common action of the whole People of God, and not merely an act of the ordained which the people observe. This was one of the most significant principles of the Liturgical Movement, and one that we are still seeking to realize in its full implications.

Along with this recovered liturgical principle, it was inevitable that questions would be raised about the role of the ordained ministers. Many people were, for example, accustomed to referring to the priest as the "celebrant" at the Eucharist. But this custom was questioned when it was realized that all of the assembly, all of the gathered people, are the celebrants of the liturgy.[3] The people are then active participants in the liturgical action rather than passive observers of what the clergy do. The role of the priest is therefore more that of a "presider" over the liturgical action which all—the full assembly including clergy—are gathered to celebrate together.

When the word "presider" first began to appear in parish bulletins for the Sunday Eucharist, it often provoked a negative reaction—on the surface for a very good reason. The word "presider" (or occasionally "president") suggested an image of a leader of an organization, or perhaps of a chairman at a meeting of a Board of Directors. This use of the term is certainly familiar to us. But then it was discovered that in fact the title "presider" is the earliest term known to us to be used in the Church for the person who would be the pastoral leader of the community, usually the bishop.[4] The

3. The words "active participation" were often used in reference to the role of the laity in the liturgy. As liturgical theologians reflected on the implication of those words, an awareness emerged that the term celebrant should not be limited to the ministry of the presider since it is the entire assembly who are "celebrants" in the liturgical action.

4. See Justin Martyr, *I Apology 67:3–7*, in *Prayers of the Eucharist: Early and Reformed*, R.C.D. Jasper and G.J. Cuming, eds., 3rd ed. (New York: Pueblo Publishing Co., 1987), 25–30.

ministry of presiding at the Eucharist and at other sacramental rites was grounded in pastoral care, in general oversight of the local community.[5]

To see the "presider" in relationship to the gathered people for a common action calls for an important shift in the general understanding of the nature of the liturgy itself. The earlier understanding of the liturgy, in which the ordained priest was the dominant figure, had shaped the liturgical sense of both clergy and laity for many centuries.[6] The usual posture of the celebrant during that period was with his back to the people, standing while the people now knelt, so that the people could not even see the gestures he used during the course of the Eucharistic Prayer.

During this same extended period, there occurred an important theological shift that placed an increasing emphasis on the role of the priest along with a decline in the participatory role of the gathered laity. This emphasis on the priest as the one—the only one—who "confects the Sacrament" and who was often the only communicant, contributed to an increasing elaboration of the priest's ritual gestures, particularly in the context of the

---

5. Cf. Hervé-Marie Legrand, "The Presidency of the Eucharist According to the Ancient Tradition," in Kevin Seasoltz, ed., *Living Bread, Saving Cup* (Collegeville, MN: Liturgical Press, 1982), 196–221.

6. See my article "The Shape of Liturgical Formation: Vertical/ Horizontal, Horizontal/Vertical," in *Sewanee Theological Review*, 52/1 (2008), 33–47.

Eucharistic Prayer. It had become virtually his private prayer. Whereas the earliest evidence indicates that the posture of the presider was simply one of raised hands during the proclamation of the Prayer, this powerful simplicity had given way gradually to an extremely complex pattern of signs of the cross and pointing to or touching the elements of bread and wine.[7]

As candidates for ordination were either instructed by the rector of their home parish, or else by a faculty member, in the ritual actions of the Eucharistic Prayer, there was no model that could be called "normative," since these patterns often varied enormously. Clergy who were inclined toward a more Catholic sense of ritual tended to use ritual gestures with much greater frequency than those whose orientation was more within the Evangelical tradition.

The problem that often arose, whatever model a priest had adopted, was that, as I observed time and time again, this model became a lifetime commitment. Differences in the size of a church building, or the character of a particular liturgical celebration or event, or even the difference of a simple said celebration as contrasted with the primary liturgy of a Sunday morning—these had little if any

---

7. A very useful overview of this question may be found in: John K. Leonard and Nathan D. Mitchell, *The Postures of the Assembly during the Eucharistic Prayer* (Chicago: Liturgy Training Publications, 1994).

impact on what gestures a priest did when he presided at the liturgy. When the Episcopal Church affirmed the ordination of women, I hoped at first that women might offer a fresh understanding of the presider's role, but in general they adopted the same norm as the ordained men in my experience.

On one occasion, I was assisting a bishop at an ordination, and when we arrived at the Eucharistic Prayer, I had been placed at the bishop's right hand. During the Prayer, I noticed that the bishop had an extremely elaborate pattern of gestures—in fact, his hands seemed to be in motion from one gesture to the next until finally the consecrated Elements were lifted up and the people responded "Amen." A student of mine who was in the congregation that day told me afterwards that there was a look of wonder on my face throughout the Prayer, which, I assured him, was not my intention. In the sacristy after the service, I wanted, tactfully I hoped, to bring up the matter with the bishop, and I commented, "I noticed, bishop, that during the Eucharistic Prayer you have a very elaborate pattern of gestures." He replied, "Yes, that is the way I have done it for twenty-five years." I doubted that anyone had taught him what I had observed, but whatever he had learned had become simply an elaborate routine which he now did automatically, without any conscious, critical attention.

Over the years I have had the privilege of

training countless seminarians about this aspect of liturgical responsibility, and I have constantly affirmed that whatever ritual pattern they choose to use, they should know what they are doing and why they are doing it. Presiding on "automatic pilot" does not foster a thoughtful celebration of the liturgy. If one is to be intentional about this aspect of a liturgical celebration, one must be conscious of a great many external factors, perhaps most significantly what a person in the congregation sees and understands the presider to be doing. I continue to see presiders perform gestures about which little or no reflection has been done: these may have personal meaning for them, but what the congregation sees is quite different. We shall consider several examples of this situation later in this book. There is no question that when a liturgy is celebrated "facing the people," this intentionality becomes all the more important.

My work in this area has led me to ask, "How did these various ritual practices originate? What was the reason for them in the first place?" Liturgical research, which has been a primary benefit of the Liturgical Movement, has given us historical perspectives to these often-unasked questions. I believe that for most clergy, the rubrics are simply *there*— they are imprinted on our awareness through countless experiences of the liturgical rites: we tend to think, without critical consideration, that this is simply how the rite is done. But the idea of liturgical directions or ritual norms attached to particular rites did not originate with the rites themselves. Our earliest liturgical documents give us texts for the liturgy, but tell us nothing at all about how a rite was to be celebrated. We are coming to a deeper awareness that there is a *performative* aspect to a liturgical celebration which has a significance beyond what we usually associate, for example, with a theatrical performance. The performative aspect of the liturgy is more than mere representation: it *effects* what it *signifies*—it embodies the sacramental reality in tangible form. This perspective inevitably raises the question of ritual practices: what was done, and what were these practices understood to *do?*

CHAPTER 3

Earliest
Evidence

OUR EARLIEST LITURGICAL TEXTS ARE found in what are known as *libelli*— that is, "little books"—which were brief written documents in which we find some of the texts used at a particular liturgy, as, for example, a collect written for the commemoration of a particular saint. These texts might have been originally intended for use only on that one occasion. The author of such a text was perhaps the bishop who was to preside at that liturgy.[1] But these doc-

---

1. Cyrille Vogel, *Medieval Liturgy: An Introduction to the Sources,* revised and translated by William G. Storey and Niels Krogh Rasmussen (Washington, DC: The Pastoral Press, 1986), 31–38, esp. 37–38.

uments contained only texts; they gave no indication of any ritual actions that were to accompany the texts. In due course, these *libelli* gave way, for obvious practical reasons, to collections of texts for the liturgical rites. Known as *sacramentaries*, these collections were primarily of texts used at celebrations of the Eucharist. They contained the texts the presider would say.

At this early period, it was normally the bishop—the chief pastor—who would preside; delegation to presbyters took place only on rare occasions as necessary. Apart from the reading of Scripture, which was a fundamental part of every liturgical celebration, much of the liturgy drew upon an oral tradition that only came to be written down as the Church expanded in size and the bishops began to delegate more normatively their role as presider. At the Council of Nicaea (325 AD), it was decided that this delegation should be given only to the presbyters and not to deacons, who already carried significant pastoral responsibilities. It was through this delegation to the presbyterate that the pastoral care of specific congregations passed to presbyters, who thus came to share in the sacramental and priestly ministry of the bishops.

What then were the ritual actions that came to be associated with the liturgical rites? It was only in the seventh century that a new type of liturgical document developed which appears to be the source for the prescribing of specific ritual actions. This new document was known as an *Ordo*.[2] During the past century, a substantial number of such ancient *Ordines* have been published, giving us descriptions of a wide variety of rites.[3] The most influential of these is the document known as *Ordo Romanus Primus* ("The First Roman Ordo," hereafter *ORP*).[4] This document, reliably dated to about 650 AD, gives us descriptive details of a celebration of the Eucharist on Easter morning by the Bishop of Rome, in the Church of Santa Maria Maggiore in Rome. It is believed to give us an accurate description of this liturgy in the seventh century, and is significant because it gives us details concerning the Western Roman Rite in what we may call its classical form.

Yet even in the case of *ORP*, we are not given details about any ritual gestures used by the bishop during the course of the Eucharistic Prayer. Rather, it is a description of a major public event. Detailed descriptions, therefore, are concerned with major rituals related to the rite: the gathering of the bread and wine from the people, and later the

2. In modern use, this term is often used to refer to a liturgical calendar, so it is important to be aware of the difference.

3. Michel Andrieu, *Les Ordines Roman du Haut Moyen Age* (Specilegium Sacrum Lovanensis, Etudes et Documents Fascicule 23, 5 vv., Louvain, 1948).

4. Alan Griffiths, ed., *Ordo Romanus Primus*. Latin Text and Translation with Introduction and Notes. Joint Liturgical Studies 73 (London: The Alcuin Club, 2012).

process for the breaking of those loaves, now consecrated, in preparation for communion. This ordo is
concerned not so much with what we have come to
think of as ceremonial as it is a guide to the practical aspects of this event.

So the question remains: what did the presider
do with regard to ritual gestures during the course
of the proclamation of the Eucharistic Prayer?
There is no evidence that he *did* anything, other
than that he stood with hands uplifted in what
was known as the *orans*—the posture for prayer.
Indeed, this prayer posture may well have been used
by the people as well as by the bishop.[5] During the
Prayer, the people would have remained standing,
since kneeling was understood to be a penitential
posture inappropriate during a celebration of the
Eucharist. As far as we know, no gestures such as
the sign of the cross had come into the rite at this
point. The only gesture by the presider which is
indicated in *ORP* comes when the bishop and his
archdeacon lift up the consecrated bread and wine
during the singing of the doxology at the conclusion of the Prayer.

Why, then, was such a document written? An
over-simplified answer would betray the underlying political and social context in which the
Church found itself. An extended period of political

5. Cf. John K. Leonard and Nathan D. Mitchell, *The Postures of the
Assembly*, 23–26.

disorder seems to have created a desire among both civic and ecclesiastical leaders to move into a more stable ordering of both Church and society. The Church in Rome was admired because of its association with the apostles Peter and Paul who were buried there. For the Western Church, Rome had become a city of pilgrimage and its liturgical traditions, which had been definitively influenced by St. Gregory the Great (+604), were looked to as models for Christian corporate prayer.

We can only speculate as to how *ORP* relates to this larger context. It was written at some point during the decades after the death of Pope Gregory, thus at a time when the texts of the liturgy had taken on a definitive form.[6] *ORP* describes an established papal model for the Eucharist, what was known as a "stational liturgy," when on major feasts (or fasts) the pope would preside at a liturgy at a designated church within the city of Rome. These were major civic events of the Christian community in Rome.

One possible explanation for the origin of the *Ordines* is that admiration for the Roman Rite had a significant impact upon pilgrims from northern Europe. This admiration of the liturgies of the city of Rome led them to be seen as models which would

---

6. The Gelasian (590 AD) and Gregorian (595 AD) sacramentaries established the rites for both presbyteral and episcopal eucharistic celebrations.

serve to correct the often chaotic liturgical situation in the north. For that, however, more was required than merely the texts of the rites. There was thus a need for a liturgical document other than the *sacramentaries*, which, as we have noted, included only the liturgical texts. The *ordines*, which supplied descriptions of those rites, filled that need.

At a later stage, through a complex process of evolution, these two sources became fused in yet another liturgical book, the missal. The development of this new type of liturgical book also reflected the fact that the Roman Rite had, as it had come to a dominant position in northern Europe, incorporated significant texts and practices that were drawn from the local non-Roman traditions. The missal was thus a "fused" liturgical book, combining both ritual directions and texts, while including texts drawn from both the Roman Rite and from local sources.[7] It is in the missal that we find the first evidence of *rubrics*.

The missionary aspect of the life of the Church in Frankish lands meant that often the liturgy was celebrated in the presence of people who had until recently been pagans, and with whom little or no catechetical teaching had taken place. Often they had been baptized simply because their ruler had made a decision to adhere to the Church. We

---

7. Alan Griffiths gives a useful brief survey of these developments in his Introduction to *Ordo Romanus Primus*, 4–24.

should not underestimate the degree to which pagan religious attitudes were now melded with the "new religion." In this context, the celebration of the liturgy became in a real sense the private domain of the ordained priests, since it was celebrated in a language that was generally foreign to the people—that is, the language of the Roman Rite, Latin—and before a congregation whose participation may have been at the behest of local rulers.

Because of a strong emphasis on the unworthiness of sinners in the preaching at that time, lay communion was infrequent, so that generally only the priest received the consecrated Bread and Wine. Lay participation gradually shifted into a "piety of vision," which was deemed to be the appropriate mode of reception for laity. This "piety of vision" became linked to a new ritual action, namely an "elevation" of the consecrated bread over the head of the priest after the Words of Institution had been said. Some theologians accepted this as a substitute for actual communion: it was called *manducatio per visum*, that is, "eating by sight."[8]

The impact of this situation upon liturgical norms was tremendous. What had been sung in a participatory liturgy was now said by only one

---

8. Cf. Miri Rubin, *Corpus Christi. The Eucharist in Late Medieval Culture* (Cambridge: Cambridge University Press, 1991), 49–82. The elevation was introduced in the late twelfth century.

ordained minister, the priest, as contrasted with the multiple ministries characteristically involved in the liturgies in a major urban center such as Rome. Rather than an important public event, the Eucharist—now generally called "the Mass"—became virtually a private act entirely dependent upon the priest.[9]

The development of the missal, in which all the texts were found within a single volume, was a perfect embodiment of this liturgical model. The priest had become the only celebrant and often the only communicant. One can scarcely imagine a model in greater contrast to the Eucharist of the First Roman *Ordo*.

It is in this context that the gestures of the priest during the Eucharistic Prayer developed a life of their own. The altar missals from the ninth century onward show an increasing incorporation of gestures such as signs of the cross into the rituals associated with the Prayer. The rite was becoming an act of priestly piety in which the people had no essential role: the Prayer was to be said in virtual silence, inaudible except to an acolyte who might serve the priest, and who would, as this new model took its definitive late medieval form, ring a bell at the "moment of consecration" so that the people

---

9. The name "Mass" is believed to have originated in the concluding dismissal at the liturgy when the deacon (or priest) said, "Ite missa est," that is, "Go forth, you are dismissed."

might look up and adore as the Elements were lifted over the head of the priest.

In the Western Church this "moment" came to be linked precisely to the *Verba Christi*—the words which Jesus said at the last supper, "This is my body . . . this is my blood." The liturgical historian Gary Macy offers us a description of the elevation and the fervor of the people in seeing the consecrated Host on the Feast of Corpus Christi in the thirteenth century. He writes:

> God's own Body and Blood are
> recreated on the altar and raised
> on high for all to see. A black velvet
> cloth is draped behind the altar to
> show up more clearly the small white
> host. At the moment of elevation, the
> crowd milling around the outside of
> the great doors rush forward to see,
> jostling and crowding, while they
> pray for the special benefits they
> know will come from seeing the Lord
> of lords that day.[10]

It was the "work" of the priest in saying Mass to make this "eucharistic miracle" available for the people to see; only a priest had this power.

As this emphasis on the role of the priest became established as the norm, we have historical evidence

---

10. Gary Macy, *The Banquet's Wisdom* (New York: Paulist Press, 1992), 126.

that a concern emerged that all priests should, at a celebration of the Eucharist, perform the same gestures. One factor behind this concern was the fact that many priests, especially outside of the urban centers, were poorly educated and often served in villages in which the people were illiterate. One can understand that bishops were concerned to have some assurance, given this situation, that the priest was doing what the Church intended and that the sacramental Presence of the Lord was being adequately and uniformly confected.

As we have observed earlier, new types of liturgical documents emerge in response to new situations or needs. The need for a standard ritual model to which all priests were expected to conform led to the creation of such a new type of liturgical document. What turned out to be the most influential response to this need was a document written by an English Franciscan, Haymo of Faversham (c. 1200–1243). Haymo was already famous as a preacher and teacher at the University of Paris when he entered the Franciscan Order in 1224, becoming Master General in 1240, just three years before his death. He led an unusually active life, but his importance for us with regard to the liturgy rests upon his treatise titled *Indutus planeta*, in which he spelled out in minute detail every posture and gesture required of a priest in the celebration of the Mass.

Haymo seems to have been considered an expert on liturgical matters: Pope Gregory IX called upon him to revise the Roman Breviary, which was authorized in 1241 for use in all of the churches of Rome, and which later became the official breviary for all the clergy of the Western Church. On the basis of this fact alone, it is clear that a high level of liturgical expertise was attributed to Haymo. Thus it is no surprise that his treatise on the ceremonial of the priest at Mass was eventually incorporated into altar missals and became the standard all priests were expected to follow in the Western Church. This ritual model for the manual acts of a priest during the Eucharistic Prayer continued as the general norm for bishops and priests up until the Reformation attacks on this entire approach to the liturgy as nothing more than "the inventions of men."

CHAPTER 4

After the Reformation

WHEN WE SEEK THE SOURCE for the gestures that a presider uses in the celebration of the Eucharistic Prayer, we need to keep Haymo and his *Industus planeta* in mind. On the whole, there has been relatively little discussion of the origin and development of this aspect of liturgical rituals. Priests inclined toward a minimal use of gesture have, within the Anglican tradition, not generally turned to any auxiliary documents, whereas those influenced by the Catholic revival which began in the nineteenth century often looked beyond the minimal rubrics of the *Book of Common Prayer* and incorporated manual acts from the Roman missal—and thus from Haymo's model—adapted to the Anglican rites.

The pattern described by Haymo in the thirteenth century was, as we have observed, the primary model used in England from that time until the Reformation three centuries later, and thus served as the primary departure point for liturgical developments in England during the early decades of the Reformation. The ritual adjustments of the first *Book of Common Prayer* (1549) were essentially a modification of the rituals identified with the Roman Rite which had dominated liturgical practice for centuries. Archbishop Cranmer did not start from scratch in his liturgical projects: he worked primarily from the medieval sources, especially the Sarum Rite, which had been the most important Use of the Roman Rite in England.[1]

In due course the English liturgical reforms went much further under the influence of such Continental reformers as Martin Bucer (1491–1551) and Peter Martyr Vermigli (1499–1562). Cranmer asked for the opinions of both these reformers, then living in England, about the 1549 book and how it should be revised. In 1547, the death of King Henry

---

1. In chapter 7, we shall discuss more fully the subsequent evolution of these rituals in more recent Anglican practice.

VIII, whose liturgical views were very traditional, opened the door to liturgical reforms more deeply influenced by the principles of the Continental reformers.

Both Bucer and Vermigli submitted proposals for the revision of the 1549 BCP, the majority of which were concerned with a radical simplification of the rites. Among them was a rejection of the use of the chasuble, which was associated with the late medieval theology of the Mass, in which, in the understanding of many clergy and lay people, each celebration of the Mass was understood to be a repetition of Calvary. Since the chasuble had become the normative vestment for the Mass, worn only by bishops and priests and only in the celebration of that liturgy, the chasuble became for the reformers a tangible symbol of the eucharistic theology which they rejected—that in each celebration of the Mass the sacrifice of Jesus in his death on the cross was repeated.

As a consequence to the reformers' rejection of this teaching, issues surrounding the theology and practice of the Eucharist became a primary area of conflict in the rejection of Roman Catholic authority. The 1552 BCP was an attempt to recover the original simplicity naively attributed to patterns of worship in "the early Church." Certainly it marked a significant simplification of the ritual gestures that had been characteristic of the late medieval eucharistic rite. Of all the authorized prayer books in the history of Anglicanism, the 1552 book went the farthest in the direction of the theological priorities associated with Calvinism, and most particularly as these came to be interpreted by the English Puritans. But this line of development was cut short by the accession to the throne of Queen Elizabeth I in 1558.

The *Book of Common Prayer* of 1559 was an important part of what is known as "the Elizabethan Settlement," and was seen as a victory for the moderate reformers who wanted to maintain the traditional liturgy in opposition to the more extreme group from Geneva, who favored a rejection of formal rites for Calvin's "Scripture only" model. Although the 1559 book marked a restoration of the book of 1552 in many ways, there were a few important changes.

From a theological perspective, the most significant of these were two changes related to an affirmation of the Real Presence of Christ in the Eucharist. These were the restoration of the Words of Administration from the 1549 rite: "The Body of our Lord Jesus Christ . . ." and "The Blood of our Lord Jesus Christ . . ." were combined with those of 1552, "Take and eat this in remembrance . . ." and "Drink this in remembrance . . ."—thus, although reflecting two very different theologies of the Eucharist, nevertheless recovering the phrases associated with the higher eucharistic doctrine, now placed within an ambivalent context.

A second change, also related to the understanding of the Eucharist, was the removal of the so-called "Black Rubric," which had been inserted at the last minute into the book of 1552 to ensure that the familiar Anglican practice of kneeling for communion should not be interpreted to imply any adoration of "the sacramental bread and wine," nor of "any real and essential presence there being of Christ's natural flesh and blood."[2] The tension within Anglicanism on this point reflects the post-Reformation concern about the meaning of "the Real Presence of Christ" and the rejection of what had emerged in the late Middle Ages as a grossly carnal interpretation of transubstantiation.[3]

It is much more common in the sacramental theology of our own time to speak of the various modes of the Presence of Christ: in the Church, in the proclamation of the word, in the prayers of the people, and yes, in the sacrament of the Eucharist. But in the sixteenth century, the 'weight' of medieval theology and, above all, ritual practice, had brought an almost exclusive focus upon the Presence of Christ

2. Cf. G.J. Cuming, *A History of Anglican Liturgy*, 85–86. Cf. the modified version, which was recovered in the 1662 BCP, in Paul V. Marshall, *Prayer Book Parallels, Vol. 1* (New York: Church Hymnal Corp., 1989), 388.

3. Cf. James F. McCue, "The Doctrine of Transubstantiation from Berengar to Trent," in *Harvard Theological Review*, 61 (1968), 385–430.

in the consecrated gifts of Bread and Wine, and a correction was deemed necessary. It was this question that the various reformers addressed in a multitude of ways—not all of them satisfactory. But that this reaction would take place was inevitable.

Theological and Apologetical Writings

By the end of the reign of Elizabeth I in 1603, the Puritans had been effectively expelled from the mainstream of English church life. But Puritan criticism of the *Book of Common Prayer* and its "papist rites" led to a flourishing period of Anglican apologetical reflection upon prayer book forms of worship. Richard Hooker (1554–1600) famously identified Anglicanism as the *via media* between Rome and Geneva. His decision to address the Puritan views was the primary motivation for writing his major work, *Of the Laws of Ecclesiastical Polity*. Much of Hooker's concern in this work was to offer a rationale for the *Book of Common Prayer*, which in turn established the context for a remarkable series of apologetical writings in defense of "the Anglican way,'" with particular attention to liturgical practices.

Throughout the seventeenth century, a long succession of writers continued to defend the ritual forms of the prayer book in opposition to the ritual excesses of Rome on the one hand and "the squalid sluttery of fanatic conventicles" on the other.[4] A great deal of preaching on this subject also took place, as in the series of sermons by the Rev. Dr. Thomas Bisse (1675–1731) on "The Beauty of Holiness in the Common-Prayer." This apologetical stance also flowed over into the American colonies where Samuel Johnson of Connecticut, an infamous "Yale convert" of 1722, addressed the New England Puritans with similar preaching and teaching in defense of the "middle way" of the English Church.[5]

The ideal for these writers was that the liturgy should offer edification, order, and uniformity, and that the rites should unfold within a framework of beauty: beauty of language, beauty of ritual, and beauty of space. This ideal was summed up in a description of Bishop George Bull (1634–1710), who "all through his life emphasized the necessity of a reverent, distinct, and leisurely reading, if the full beauty of the rite was to be brought out."[6] But this concern about liturgical worship must not be misunderstood with regard to actual ritual practices. The ritualism of the Catholic Revival within Anglicanism lay a full century in the future.

---

4. From a pamphlet written by Simon Patrick, and quoted in: P.E. More and F.L. Cross, in *Anglicanism* (London: S.P.C.K., 1935), 12. Also see the list of authors given by G.W.O. Addleshaw in *The High Church Tradition* (London: Faber and Faber, 1941), pp. 30–32.

5. Cf. P. Kingsley Smith, "Samuel Johnson of Connecticut," in The Anglican Theological Review, Vol. 39 (1957), pp. 217-229, esp. 222-3.

6. G.W.O. Addleshaw, *The High Church Tradition*, 66.

In the seventeenth century, ritual practices were remarkably simple. For example, bowing to the altar when one entered a church or went forward for communion was practiced in some circles, but was looked upon by others with great suspicion. It is difficult for us to grasp today the degree to which the sixteenth century reaction against Roman Catholicism produced among the English people a tendency to see any ritual action or the use of a "fixed form" as an expression of "popery." For the Puritans, even the use of the Lord's Prayer was condemned as a fixed form that inhibited the free working of the Holy Spirit. For them, authentic prayer was spontaneous. It was against these extreme anti-ritualistic views that the defense of the prayer book was aimed. The apologetic writings referred to seem to have been more concerned with the dignity and order of a service than with the kind of ritual preoccupations that would develop a century later.

The Impact of the Catholic Revival

The Oxford Movement began as a reaction to the abysmal state into which the English Church had fallen by the beginning of the nineteenth century. Throughout the previous century, government policies with regard to the Church of England had come to model those identified with Erastianism, that is, the principle that the State had supreme authority over the Church and held regulatory authority over religious matters. In this model, the Church becomes rather like "a department of religious affairs." For the leaders of the Oxford Movement, this situation had become intolerable and so, in their teaching and above all in the publication of their *Tracts for the Times*, they called for the restoration of the integrity and autonomy of the Church. It was for this reason that the Oxford leaders were drawn to a reaffirmation of the "apostolic succession" of the bishops, since it was through this succession that the bishops were placed in a line that directly connected them to the apostles and thus to Jesus Christ. This claim was an appeal for the autonomy of the Church to regulate its life rather than to be dominated by the secular priorities of government officials.

In addition to the subjection of the Church to the control of the State, the effects of the Enlightenment also had significant impact upon the English Church. Advances in scientific knowledge were thought to stand in opposition to traditional Christian doctrine. The Enlightenment emphasized that reason alone could be the basis of truth. The effect of this was a general disparagement of the mystical element of religion, and with it an extreme marginalization of the sacramental and liturgical aspects of Christian faith

and practice. God was seen to work through natural law, producing a kind of deistic form of
Christianity in which the sacraments had no place.
A dry formalism had become characteristic of the
public worship of the Church.

The focus of the Movement during its first phase
was thus historical and theological. The Church
was affirmed as God's instrument in human history. Concern for the sacramental life of the
Church was based upon a sense of the sacramental
nature of the Church as a whole, and was not at
first concerned about specifically ritual matters.
But the Oxford leaders' emphasis upon the corporate nature of the Church became a key factor in
their program. In one of his sermons, John Henry
Newman said:

> Christ has lodged his blessings in
> the body collectively to oblige them
> to meet *together* if they would gain
> grace each for himself. The body is
> the first thing and each member in
> particular the second. The body is not
> made up of individual Christians, but
> each Christian has been made such
> in his turn by being *taken into the*
> *body.*
>
> *(Sermon 213)*

With this theological perspective, the Oxford
Movement leaders took a powerful stand against

the rationalism of the Enlightenment, but also against the lack of a vital sense of the corporate nature of the Church which was characteristic of the Evangelicals. The Evangelicals had pointed to the dry rationalism that had come to dominate the Church of England, but it was through the leaders at Oxford that an understanding of the Church as the mystical Body of Christ was restored.[7]

7. See my article, "The Tractarian Liturgical Inheritance Re-Assessed," in Geoffrey Rowell, ed., *Tradition Renewed* (London: Darton, Longman and Todd, 1986), 110–19.

CHAPTER 5

The Liturgical
Act

I F THIS CHAPTER WERE TITLED "The Liturgical Rite," readers might assume that it would be a discussion of the texts of particular rites, as for example, the rites of the *Book of Common Prayer*, or perhaps how rites are structured for public worship. But the use of the word "act" points us to a deeper level, to factors that form the underlying aspects of liturgical rites in general: how those rites embody the common understanding of how such a rite will be performed in a particular time and context.

For many centuries, the Church operated with a liturgical understanding of the ordained clergy as the primary agents of the liturgical action and the gathered laity as the receivers of those liturgical ministries. This basic attitude was true whether we are thinking of specifically Anglican rites, of Roman Catholic rites, or of the models that were in use in Protestant communities. In other words, this clericalized understanding of how liturgical rites were to be celebrated was common ground even for a variety of religious traditions, and even when the various religious traditions were most hostile to each other. It was the clergy who had authority over the public worship of the Christian community. That was the common understanding for clergy and laity alike.

Within this model, Christian piety was conceived in essentially individual or inward terms. That inward piety had a type of external expression in the official public rites of a particular church. In a sense, piety was understood as a private act on the part of an individual Christian; a private act which might take place in the context of public ceremonial. If a number of people were gathered together in a church building for worship, what took place were multiple private acts of Christian piety occurring simultaneously.

One important example of this individualization of the mode of participation was perhaps most clearly embodied in a practice common among Roman Catholic laity prior to the Second Vatican Council. While the Mass was celebrated in virtual silence by a priest at the altar, the members of the congregation would individually be praying the rosary or other private devotions. The "participation" expected of them was to observe the priest at the altar as he was "offering the Sacrifice on their behalf," and specifically to look at him when he said the consecratory Words of Institution and then lifted the Elements of bread and wine over his head in two dramatic elevations ritually underscored by the ringing of bells. The role of the people was then to gaze upon the now transubstantiated Elements and to say to themselves the words of Thomas, "my Lord and my God." Since communion was generally infrequent, this gazing upon the Elements after consecration constituted a kind of "piety of vision," which, as we observed earlier, gave the laity an alternative mode for communion with God.

Yet even if we see this as a clear example of an essentially private act in the context of a public ceremonial, it was in other ways often true as well in Protestant services at which the individuals were expected to listen to the preacher and to receive from the sermon the spiritual nourishment needed for their daily lives. This amounted to a kind of "passive participation" through listening, essentially a word/mind interaction. Physical participation was as minimal as one can conceive.

In those Anglican parishes where the liturgical principles of the prayer book were practiced by people and clergy alike, the liturgical rites— whether the Eucharist or Morning Prayer—were celebrated as a corporate action, involving the people together with their parish priest. I make this claim with caution, however, since it is possible to perform rites that presume lay participation, but in which the clerical domination of the liturgy has been maintained and in which the people are essentially passive, although they may respond "And with thy spirit" at certain points in the rite. "Active participation" implies a much deeper form of participation than merely the declaration of a few responses.

The danger with even corporate liturgical rites is that they may touch the surface of the people's experience and yet not influence their liturgical piety in depth. It is the purpose of this chapter to present the meaning of the liturgical act by holding both of these dimensions together, that is, both the external rite and the integration of the rite in the faith life of the gathered community. For that to happen, a liturgy must be more than watched or heard: it must connect at the deepest levels with the realities of the worshiper's life.

I want to suggest that the clericalization of the

liturgy—the focus of the entire liturgical action in the ministry of the priest—is the historical point of origin of the alienation of the laity from authentic participation in liturgical celebrations. As we observed in chapter 2, the watershed on these matters, the historical point at which the various factors came into a new alignment, occurred in the thirteenth century. Obviously, many of the developments of the preceding centuries had led in this direction. But it was during the pontificate of Pope Innocent III (1198–1216), in connection with his zeal for much-needed reform in the Church, that the focus of all sacramental authority came to be definitively given to the ordained priesthood. This was affirmed in the Church's canon law at the Fourth Lateran Council in 1215.

At the time of the Reformation in the sixteenth century, in spite of the Reformers' rejection of what they called the *hocus pocus* performed by the priest in the Mass,[1] the issue of the domination of public worship by the clergy was never effectively addressed. One can suggest, of course, that to some degree this was a consequence of generally low standards of education except for a privileged minority, or it may have been a result of the

---

1. Although the claim has been disputed, the origin of the words *hocus-pocus* are thought by some to reflect anti-Roman Catholic prejudice linked to the Words of Institution in the Canon of the Latin Mass: *"hoc est enim corpus meum"*—"This is my body." The commonly accepted meaning links it to an incantation said by a magician, which reinforces the idea of religious bias.

total loss of basic Christian formation during the preceding centuries due to the collapse of the catechumenate, which had prepared candidates for Baptism into the fifth century.

In other words, preparation for Christian living and for regular participation in the Church's worship had been a common part of the formation expected for all Christians in the Church's early centuries. The loss of the catechumenate had enormous and far-reaching consequences, so that by the sixteenth century, by which time a millennium of the gradual "inferiorization" of the laity had passed, it was taken for granted that the laity would receive no substantial catechetical education. This problem has continued to affect the life of the Church generally. One of my great teachers during my doctoral studies was the Dominican theologian André Liégé. In class one day he asked us, "What do we do if we are about to proclaim the Gospel and celebrate the eucharistic rite, but we realize that our people do not understand what any of this means?" And then with great passion he responded to his own question: "We go to them and *teach.*" But the clerical dominance of the liturgy has led many people to believe that these matters are a concern only for the ordained.

Given this inferior status of the laity, the individualistic piety of the later medieval period continued, even within the Protestant context. The role of the laity seems to have been restricted primarily to attendance at religious services which focused on evangelization and education. Listening to the sermon became the primary purpose of lay attendance; the often quite lengthy sermon *served as the basis for edification in faith*. Some of the more extreme reformers placed such emphasis on private prayer that public worship took second place, being viewed by some as a distraction from a personal life of prayer.

There is an irony in this situation on the Roman Catholic side of the same question: at the Council of Trent (1545–1563), a few bishops asked that the laity be discouraged from attending Mass, but that they should rather remain at home and say their prayers, so that the priest might offer Mass undistracted by the intrusive noises of the laity. This suggestion was not approved by the council, but even its proposal is a reminder of how non-essential laity had become. Again, a highly individualized piety on the part of both clergy and laity was understood as the Church's norm.

With its emphasis on the full participation of all the people, including children, in the celebration of the liturgy, the modern Liturgical Movement began to confront this individualized piety as inimical to the true nature of the liturgy. It claimed, in fact, that the authentic liturgical act turns that individualized piety upside down. The presence of other persons is not a distraction for the individual worshiper—whether lay or ordained—but is essential for the experience of liturgical prayer as the common prayer of faith for all the people. This was in no way intended as a denigration of the place of private prayer in the life of a Christian, but rather to suggest that a mature Christian piety requires both, and to recognize that they are different.

Ultimately it is corporate prayer that is foundational in Christian experience. Private prayer is an expression in the life of the individual Christian of the common prayer that is shared in the liturgical assembly: that common prayer shared with our sisters and brothers in Christ embodies the common ground of faith into which we have been baptized. Corporate prayer is an expression of that common life.

Characteristics of the Liturgical Act

Let us consider the basic characteristics of what we are calling 'the liturgical act.' It is first of all the common action of a gathering of people as the Body of Christ. In that action, human beings participate with their whole humanity. The liturgical act is not merely an activity of the mind in which words and ideas supply the main content. Rather, the authentic liturgical act must involve our bodies and our senses—our hearts as well as our minds. The liturgical act is thus sensual corporate prayer.

The liturgical act is also ritual prayer: it involves actions at a particular time and place. In that sense, it is rather like human play in that it gathers us in a designated context in which the content of the action is defined, and in which many of the elements of the act are known through regular repetition. It is in this regard that liturgical rites have their role in Christian worship: they link us to generations of Christians who have, like ourselves, gathered to perform these same actions of faith which embody our identity as Christians.

The liturgical act is not a random collection of diverse pieces. For several years, I collected programs from a variety of church services that I had attended. My purpose was to learn how Sunday services were structured, with particular attention to the non-liturgical traditions. Such programs are often revelatory of a local community's understanding of what it is that they are doing when they gather for public prayer. With an amazing frequency, such programs supplied only a listing of items: a hymn, a reading, a prayer, a sermon, listed as a sequence, but often with no indication as to the structural relationship among these diverse pieces. I am suggesting that liturgical celebrations stand in contrast to these generally sermon-centered models: the liturgical act is structured—there is an integral relation between its parts.

Often in my teaching over the years, I have found that an approach that is basic for me is one with which students are unfamiliar: that approach is to examine a particular liturgical celebration with an eye as to how its various constitutive elements are related to each other in an integrative way. My intention in this is that a liturgy be experienced as "whole cloth"—that the various elements be evidently connected. Often in my experience as a visitor, I have found a hymn, an anthem, or a prayer apparently "stuck in" because someone likes it. The implication is that "I like it" is a sufficient reason to include liturgical items without a serious consideration of their purpose—or lack of purpose—in the rite as a whole.

One particularly memorable example of this was an occasion when I was a visitor in a Midwestern parish on the Sunday of the Passion—thus, one week before Easter Day. I was in the area giving some lectures at a local educational institution. I did not know the members of the parish or the rector, so I had no idea what to expect when I went that Sunday morning. Since it was Passion Sunday, I assumed that the readings and music would all be related to that focus, a primary event in the Christian calendar, and that the Liturgy of the Palms would probably serve as the first part of the Passion Eucharist.

The blessing of the palms did come first. Later, after the reading of the Passion, we were told that instead of a sermon that day, we would see a play which a group had prepared. The subject of the play was "the prodigal son." This was followed by an anthem on a text drawn from the liturgy of the palms—both of these elements falling *after the reading of the Passion.* I felt that I was being hurled about in a clothes dryer: where was the focus of this liturgy?

Let us presume that the play had been well rehearsed and performed, and that the anthem was sung well: unfortunately, this is beside the point. What we experienced in the congregation that day was a series of items which, even if well done, were not integrated into the central focus of the liturgy on that day. Whoever the planners were—whether the clergy or the musicians or a lay committee— the result was so diffuse that the primary intention of this important Christian observance was obscured. We had experienced a kind of liturgical smorgasbord.

The liturgical act is not made up of a laundry list of items: it is a whole, a unity which with its particular focus invites us to contemplate one facet of the fundamental Christian mystery of God in Christ. This is why we do not sing Christmas carols at the

Easter liturgy! In its full and authentic sense, the liturgical act is formative of the people of God who have gathered for corporate prayer. In this act, the people encounter, through word and sacrament, the living God who is present and active in their lives.

In an authentic liturgical act, all the strands of Christian faith and history are brought together in a unifying focus upon a specific aspect of the Christian revelation. This is how the liturgical year plays a fundamental role in its unfolding of the faith within an annual cycle. To achieve that purpose, it seems to me that the liturgical calendar should not become too complicated. When Archbishop Thomas Cranmer simplified the calendar in the early stages of the development of the first *Book of Common Prayer*, he reacted against the overloaded state of the calendar in the later middle ages. Christians have throughout history remembered the men and women who have lived heroic lives of faith often at enormous cost to themselves. They should be remembered, but how their remembrance is related to a liturgical celebration can become quite problematic.

It would be easy to list two or three such heroes for every day of the year. This is essentially the problem that Cranmer confronted. His solution was quite radical: to reduce the calendar dramatically, limiting it to persons mentioned in Scripture, plus a short list of very popular saints. But the question of who should be commemorated has reappeared in recent decades, and we are again faced with the problem of expecting one liturgy to hold together too diverse a group of intentions. The main question is not whom to commemorate: it is quite within the capacity of the local church, ideally with guidance from the bishop's office, to form an annual list of commemorations that have significance in the life of that diocese. This might include, as an obvious example, holy persons from whom a parish or mission of the diocese takes its name. But this question can be easily resolved with appropriate diocesan leadership. Every church of the diocese does not need to observe every possible commemoration—in fact, even if this were a goal, it could not be done.

The real issue is to connect this question to the understanding of the liturgical act and the principles that were set forth earlier: the need for a certain reserve, a certain understatement, which will help to foster a clear emphasis on the primary focus of that particular liturgical celebration. The place to look first for that focus is in the Gospel reading of the day. When the Gospel reading is taken as that primary focus, the other aspects of the liturgy can be easily determined in relation to it.

The Liturgy as Icon of the Church

Often in ways not consciously intended, the manner in which a liturgy is celebrated reveals an understanding of the nature of the Church. Many of us can remember celebrations of the Eucharist in which the priest/celebrant performed all of the liturgical ministries customarily associated with the rite. By this I mean that the priest not only presided and said the Eucharistic Prayer, but he (and, of course, at that time it was always "he") also read the Gospel, and thus took the role of a deacon. Further, the priest often also read the Epistle, thus taking the ministry of a lector. At a Eucharist I attended, there was no acolyte, and so the bread and wine were placed prior to the liturgy at one corner of the altar where the priest could easily reach them for himself. The priest was thus the only *minister* of that liturgy. The late Boone Porter referred to this model of liturgical leadership as "the omnivorous priesthood."[2]

Admittedly this rather extreme example is not common, even at a said celebration. Yet not long ago when I visited a parish while passing through town on a trip, I attended the 8:00 a.m. celebration of the Eucharist, and what I have described above is exactly what was done. What struck me at the time

---

2. Cf. H.B. Porter: "A Traditional Reflection on Diaconate in Relation to 'Omnivorous Priesthood,'" in *Living Worship* 12 (9), November 1976.

was that I was probably the only person attending that day who found this pattern strange. The congregation had probably experienced that model for many years and so it had, for them, assumed a kind of "normative" status. I have often observed that when a congregation experiences a particular model of liturgical celebration over a long period, that model becomes for them the way in which they believe that the rite should be celebrated.

If we may compare this model of liturgical celebration with our understanding of the nature of the Church, the connection is quite clear. We have come a long way during the last few decades toward changing a clericalized model of ministry. The 1979 *Book of Common Prayer* clearly manifests an understanding of "ministry" that is diverse and inclusive of the numerous ministries that are normally performed by laity. Under the influence of the 1979 *Book of Common Prayer*, our models of liturgical celebration have also been reshaped so that this diverse understanding of ministry is expressed within the celebration itself, as the various actions of the rite are performed by lay members of the congregation as well as by the ordained clergy in their appropriate roles.

It is in this sense that I am suggesting that the model in which a liturgy is celebrated—that is, the familiar model that is generally repeated week after week in a parish—is reflective of how "ministry" is conceived and embodied in that community. We are pointing here to something more fundamental than simply the texts of the rite as they are printed in the *Book of Common Prayer*. It is quite possible to celebrate the same rite, using the same texts, and yet to manifest very different understandings of liturgical and sacramental ministries.

This awareness has contributed, since the 1979 BCP was authorized, to a shift away from a model in which the "celebrant" performed most if not all of the various ministries to a model in which, in most parishes, the Sunday liturgy requires a variety of ministers. This has contributed also, as we observed in chapter 2, to a change in vocabulary in which "celebrant" has often been replaced by "presider." This early title for one who leads a Christian community in its celebration of the Eucharist is found in a document written by Justin Martyr in about the year 150 AD at Rome; this is the earliest known appearance of the term. Following his description of a Baptism, Justin writes:

> Then bread and a cup of water and
> (a cup) of mixed wine are brought to
> him who presides over the brethren,
> and he takes them and sends up
> praise and glory to the Father of all
> in the name of the Son and of the

Holy Spirit and gives thanks at some
length . . .[3]

The "leader" at this time would have been the person whom we call "the bishop," in other words, the chief pastor of the community. Since Christian communities were quite small, the need had not yet arisen, as it would from the fourth century onwards, for the bishop to delegate this liturgical ministry at the Eucharist to his presbyters.

As to ritual gestures in this context, we are told only that "the presider" takes the bread and wine that have been presented to him and offers prayer over them. We may presume that the gifts were placed on a table at which the presider would stand, and that he would then raise his hands in the normal posture of prayer, the *orans*. The evidence we have suggests that all of the people, and not just the presider, would have lifted their arms during the Eucharistic Prayer. Although the presider proclaimed the Prayer, this shared posture indicates that it was being offered by all the people in union with the presider. Justin gives us no indication that the presider performed any other gestures during the course of the prayer. Such manual actions would not appear in a liturgical text until well into the early middle ages.

---

3. *First Apology 65.1*, in R.C.D. Jasper and G.J. Cuming, *Prayers of the Eucharist: Early and Reformed*, 3rd ed. (New York: Pueblo Publishing, 1980), 28.

Full lay participation in the Eucharist is thus not merely a current liturgical fashion that is being imposed upon a congregation: eucharistic celebration in which all participants are understood to be "con-celebrants" is simply an embodiment of an understanding of the nature of the Church itself. Under the leadership of the clergy of a community, it is that entire community that "celebrates" the Eucharist, each according to his or her role within the community. All these roles are complementary to each other since it is together as an assembly that all those gathered are "celebrants."

It is in this sense that the normative liturgical celebration in the Sunday Eucharist is a mirror to that community's self-understanding as "Church." The purpose of the outward signs in the liturgical rites is to embody and reveal the inner reality to which the rites point. If the rites are not to be merely a religious façade, they must be connected to the lived experience of the members, not as isolated individuals but as members of one body, the Body of Christ. The liturgical celebration, through both word and sacrament, reminds us by offering to us an ever-deepening sense of that membership. We are summoned out of a myopic focus upon ourselves into an unfolding participation in our common life as members of Christ.

Even a "renewed" liturgy does not accomplish this in a kind of automatic way. In America, religious experience has been influenced by the individualism of frontier Protestantism with its literalist orientation, creating a kind of filter that has shaped religious attitudes in this country within all religious traditions, and even for people who have rejected any form of religious practice. This filter is all the more significant because we are often unaware of its influence in our daily lives. This poses a particular challenge to those churches in which the sacraments play a significant role, for us in the Anglican tradition, but also for Roman Catholics and Lutherans. Literalism subverts the integrity of the liturgical act.

A pervasive literalist mindset stands in direct opposition to forms of worship in which symbols have a central place. As a consequence, liturgical rites may express the external aspect of a symbol, but any engagement with the inner meaning of the symbol is eroded when the rite is engaged only at a literal level. Thus when we speak of the consecrated bread and wine as the Body and Blood of Christ, a literalist mindset has a serious problem: obviously our eyes tell us that the bread and wine are not flesh and blood. So either we are forced to accept some idea of an invisible chemical change in the two elements, which is the unfortunate and erroneous interpretation given by some to the theory of transubstantiation,[4] or else we see the bread and wine merely as reminders of what Christ did for us many centuries ago, which is the teaching associated with the Swiss Reformer Ulrich Zwingli (1484-1531). Both of these views are indicative of an inability to deal with symbol in the sense taught by St. Augustine: that the bread and wine through the prayer of consecration become the outward signs of the inner reality which the consecrated Gifts offer to us: the sacramental Presence of Christ's Body and Blood.

When the fundamental symbols expressed in an authentic liturgical act take root in our daily lives, those symbols have the power to touch the deepest levels of our humanity, leading us into a path of transformation. But if the symbols are engaged only on the surface, this potential for transformation is lost. There is abundant evidence in the life of the Church that a person can be "religious," attending church every Sunday, and yet not live the faith they profess. The consequence of this is a kind of christianized veneer that is only skin deep.

The imperatives of the Gospel are proclaimed not only in the liturgical rites and their ritual symbols. Those imperatives, when they are truly *heard and accepted*, become embodied in the ways in which

---

4. See the excellent discussion of the meaning of this sacramental change in: Edward Schillebeeckx, "Transubstantiation, Transfinalization, Transignification," in K. Seasoltz, ed., *Living Bread, Saving Cup* (Collegeville, MN: Liturgical Press, 1982), 175–89.

Christians live their lives. It is in our daily lives that the authenticity of our Christian faith meets its essential test. The significance of the liturgical act is not found merely in the performance of a religious routine, no matter how beautiful that routine may be. It is found when that act yields in us the spiritual fruit that it signifies.

CHAPTER 6

The Laying-on-of-Hands

THE LAYING-ON-OF-HANDS IS THE FUNDA-MENTAL ritual gesture in all of the sacramental actions of the Church. This may seem to be a rather exaggerated claim since, as many laity and clergy would point out on the basis of their experience, it does not appear to have such a significant place in sacramental practice. The laying-on-of-hands can appear to be a rather trivial gesture.

Yet during the early centuries of Christianity, as recent scholarship has suggested, this gesture can be understood as the basic liturgical action for all the sacraments.[1] After the Great Schism between Rome and Constantinople in 1054, theological developments in each tradition—Orthodox and Roman—progressed in very distinct ways. In the West, both theology and spirituality took a firmly Christological focus, whereas the Eastern developments maintained a strong emphasis on the role of the Holy Spirit in all sacramental actions. On the basis of the earliest evidence available to us, the action of the Spirit was, from a ritual perspective, closely linked to the gesture of the laying-on-of-hands. Among scholars there is general agreement that this ritual action is the earliest manual act used by a presider in the proclamation of the Eucharistic Prayer, done as the presider said the words of the *epiclesis* or Invocation of the Holy Spirit upon the gifts of bread and wine.

This gesture was also used in other sacramental actions: in the signing of a baptismal candidate immediately after the water rite; in the rite of the laying-on-of-hands by the bishop after a candidate came out of the water (which later became separated as the rite of confirmation); in the rites for the ordination of bishops, priests, and deacons; in the declaring of forgiveness in the rite of

1. Godfrey Diekmann, O.S.B., "The Laying on of Hands: The Basic Sacramental Rite," in *Proceedings of the Twenty-Ninth Annual Convention of the Catholic Theological Society of America*, 29 (June 10–13, 1974): 339–51.

reconciliation; in the blessing of a couple at their marriage; and in both the anointing of the sick and the final anointing at the time of the death of a Christian. So it was that in these rites, the laying-on-of-hands was the single gesture common to all. It was the gesture that embodied ritually the action of the Holy Spirit in the sacramental actions of the Church. In each context, it was the prayer that indicated the specific purpose for which the Holy Spirit was being invoked, the gift or ministry which the Spirit was being asked to impart, and the grace which the Spirit was understood to bestow. We find the laying-on-of-hands in all these liturgical actions, but its specific meaning in each instance was indicated by the context in which it took place.

It was the role and action of the Holy Spirit in the Eucharistic Prayer that became a particular point of conflict between East and West. In the East, the Spirit was understood as the agent of the transformation of the gifts into the Body and Blood of Christ. The Christological emphasis in the West led to the giving of particular significance to the words of Christ at his final meal with the disciples, so that the role of the presider came gradually to be seen as an action *in persona Christi*, in the person of Christ. This gave an increasing importance to the role of the priest with a consequent diminution of the role of the laity, who gradually became merely observers of the priest's sacred act.[2]

This development created a further wedge between the theological emphases of East and West, so that the words of Christ came to be seen in the West as the primary focus in the consecration of the gifts along with the absence of any articulated consecratory role being ascribed to the Holy Spirit in the Western Eucharistic Prayer. The words of Jesus came gradually to be understood as "words of consecration"— thus placing a substantial weight, in a sense, upon a formula within the Eucharistic Prayer. This led to changes in the ritual actions of the priest which we shall consider in the next chapter. It eroded the sense commonly shared during the previous centuries that it was the entire Prayer that was consecratory. As Edward Kilmartin observed:

> Within a liturgical celebration
> particular rites or symbols are
> capable of polarizing the signification
> normally transmitted by a whole
> system of symbols. Certain symbols
> are capable of assuming the
> signification of indicating or invoking
> the whole of which they are normally
> a part. However when they are

2. We should note that this idea of the priest as "another Christ" indicates a significant narrowing of the earlier understanding that every man and woman becomes "another Christ" at the time of their Baptism.

located within the totality such a
rite or symbol does not retain its
power to transmit the whole of the
signification.[3]

Here Kilmartin helps us to understand how the
emergence of an intense verbal and ritual focus
upon the Words of Institution could assume "the
signification of . . . the whole of which they are
normally a part." This isolation of the Words from
the totality of the Prayer in the end diminished the
significance of the rest of the Prayer, and led to
a dramatic transformation of the understanding of
the Words as a warrant for the total sacramental
action into a formula of consecration in which the
eucharistic Presence was "confected" by the priest
in the context of elaborate ceremonial involving
genuflections, elevations, and bells, which drew the
full attention of the people to this moment.

Developments in Anglicanism

For Anglicans, after the separation from Rome
in the sixteenth century, this question of the role
of the Holy Spirit reemerged in developments in
eucharistic theology apart from the influence of
the Roman model, which had been the primary

3. Edward J. Kilmartin, S.J., "Response to Professor Diekmann—II,"
in *Proceedings of the Twenty-Ninth Annual Convention of the Catholic
Theological Society of America*, 357–66.

71

prayer at Mass throughout England prior to the Reformation. This recovery of the role of the Holy Spirit in the context of the eucharistic consecration, however, emerged from outside the mainstream of the Church of England.

What is known as the Non-Juror[4] Schism of the late seventeenth century was a division within the English Church when a significant percentage of Church leaders, including an Archbishop of Canterbury, separated from the Established Church on the basis of a dispute about the binding character of the oath of allegiance which the bishops and other clergy were expected to give upon the accession of a monarch. This conflict developed in connection with the replacement of James II, who was a Roman Catholic, in what is known as the Glorious Revolution of 1688, when William of Orange in The Netherlands and his wife Mary, a daughter of James II, were invited by Parliament to become the constitutional monarchs of the United Kingdom. Nine bishops of the Church of England, including the Archbishop of Canterbury William Sancroft, could not in conscience give the oath to William and Mary as long as James II was alive.

Once separated from the Church of England, some members of the Non-Jurors now felt free of

---

4. From the Latin *juro* meaning "to swear an oath," thus "not swearing." The Non-Juror Schism has been thoroughly documented in an extensive bibliography; the repetition of that material is not appropriate to this study.

their ordination obligation to use the 1662 *Book of Common Prayer*. Because of their high sacramental theology, they were generally critical of the defects they found in the 1662 prayer book. Once separated from the Established Church, they could develop eucharistic rites that reflected their theological views. Ironically, in the 1662 rite, which included much of the earlier work of Archbishop Thomas Cranmer in the 1552 BCP, the emphasis had remained on the words of Christ, although no longer seen as "consecratory" in the medieval sense, but rather as the biblical mandate upon which the communion rite was based. For the Non-Jurors, basing their teaching upon early eucharistic prayers, particularly those of the Eastern Church, this emphasis on the words of Jesus only, whether on the basis of Scripture or on the Western Christological focus, was theologically inadequate.

For the Non-Jurors, the Prayer in the 1662 prayer book was seriously defective in various ways, including our subject here, namely, the role of the Holy Spirit embodied in the Eucharistic Prayer through the laying-on-of-hands. For some of the Non-Jurors, their separation from the Established Church thus led them to reject the Roman focus as well as the official 1662 *Book of Common Prayer* and to develop a Eucharistic Prayer based upon other sources, especially prayers from the Orthodox

East with their strong emphasis upon the role of the Spirit in the eucharistic consecration.

This had far-reaching consequences for Anglicanism in the American colonies for such leaders as Samuel Johnson of Connecticut (1696–1772), who had been influenced by the Non-Juror eucharistic theology through a serious study of their documents. A commitment to this theology was instilled in Samuel Seabury by his father who had studied with Johnson. When the clergy of Connecticut elected the younger Seabury to be their bishop, he was unable to receive episcopal ordination in England because of the oath of obedience to the monarch required of all clergy in the Church of England. This led Seabury to seek ordination from the Scottish bishops, who were strong advocates of the Non-Juror eucharistic teaching. Seabury agreed to introduce the Scottish Eucharistic Prayer in the development of a new *Book of Common Prayer* (1789) for the young American church. From that time to the present, the eucharistic rites in the American prayer books (1789, 1892, 1928, and 1979) have continued to reflect this heritage.

Human Touch as Sacrament

This emphasis on the ritual of the laying-on-of-hands implies that it is much more than a trivial action. It reminds us of the enormous significance of human touch. We know this in our own experience apart from any specifically ritual context. Most of us, at one time or another, have reached out to another human being, perhaps to a person who is in acute physical or emotional pain, one who has suffered the profound loss of a loved one, or as a gesture of forgiveness more powerful than words themselves. If we can understand that, we have a fundamental insight into the importance of touch in the rituals of faith. They are sacred actions, but they are also profoundly human. We understand them through our own humanity.

It should not surprise us, therefore, that both the Old and New Testaments offer many examples of the laying-on-of-hands. In his treatise on the Holy Spirit, Saint Basil the Great (329–379) compares the unity of the Son and the Spirit in their relation to the Father as being like the right and left hands of God.[5] For me, this is a wonderful image of the hand as symbolic agent—an agent that effects what it wills. As we have observed, in human experience the hand is a kind of "natural symbol": it embodies a communication from one person to another, an affirmation of the humanity of the other person. This is why, for me, the report of Jesus touching a leper has such significance.[6]

5. St. Basil the Great, *On the Holy Spirit* (Crestwood, NY: St. Vladimir's Seminary Press, 2001). See especially chapter 16, nos. 37–40, pp. 60–67.
6. Cf. Matthew 8:2–3; Mark 1:40–42; Luke 5:12–13.

Jesus did not remain aloof and bless him from afar, this person who was viewed by most people as an "untouchable." The act of touching embodies Jesus and thus communicates the healing power that Jesus willed for the leper. The hand of Jesus was an extension of himself. As Fr. Diekmann notes, the touch of Jesus "is such a power-laden gesture that it effects what it signifies."[7] The gesture is thus sacramental in that it embodies the Church's understanding of "sacrament"—it is 'performative', an action that effects the grace that it signifies.

A strong association of the action of the Holy Spirit with the laying-on-of-hands emerged very early in Christian sacramental practice. An early New Testament example of this is found at Acts 19:2–6. There we are told that Paul is at Ephesus where he found disciples who had not received the Holy Spirit. We are told that these disciples were baptized and that Paul then laid his hands upon them, "and the Holy Spirit came upon them."[8] The same link between the laying-on-of-hands and the action of the Holy Spirit may be seen in what the Church came to call "ordination" or the appointment of members of the Church to the work of special forms of ministry or leadership as in the case

---

7. Diekmann, "The Laying on of Hands," 345.
8. Acts 19:2–6.

of "the seven"[9] or of the commissioning of Barnabas and Saul.[10]

In spite of such evidence, we must acknowledge that eventually in both the Eastern and Western Churches, the laying-on-of-hands came to be eclipsed in the evolution of sacramental practice. We find examples of its place being taken by an anointing that was interpreted separately from the laying-on-of-hands as a sign of strengthening or healing. In the Eastern Church, however, the theological emphasis on the role of the Holy Spirit in the sacraments was maintained. The treatise by St. Basil the Great is an important expression of this emphasis, which continued as a major characteristic in Eastern theology.

The virtual loss of the laying-on-of-hands in Western practice offers us an important insight into what we might call the marginalization of the role of the Spirit in Western theology in general, and quite specifically in relation to the theology of the Eucharist. As was noted earlier, in the Roman Catholic eucharistic rite, the Great Thanksgiving, generally called the Roman Canon, lacks any specifically stated action of the Holy Spirit upon the consecration of the gifts.

Amazingly, this loss extended even into the rites of ordination where, one would have thought, the

9. Acts 6:6.
10. Acts 13:1–3.

biblical witness alone would have secured the centrality of the laying-on-of-hands with prayer. Yet in the teaching of St. Thomas Aquinas (1225–1274) on ordination, he says that giving of the chalice and paten to the ordinand is the primary ritual that effects ordination. This offers us additional evidence that by the late middle ages the ministerial role of a priest had come to be narrowly defined in his "power" to celebrate the Mass and to "confect" the sacrament of Christ's Body and Blood.

On this question it is important to note that one of the major accomplishments of Archbishop Cranmer may be found in the ordination rites that he crafted in 1550. In these he restored the absolute centrality of the laying-on-of-hands with prayer as the primary ritual focus. In the Roman Church this restoration of the original focus of ordination did not come until the twentieth century. It was Pope Pius XII (1876–1958) who determined with regard to Roman Catholic rites that the laying-on-of-hands is the primary act, but this affirmation was made within the context of the still-underdeveloped theology of the Spirit in the Roman Church.

At the Second Vatican Council, it was the Orthodox, Anglican, and other observers who noted the virtual absence of an emphasis on the work of the Holy Spirit in the council's documents. At the time, the response to this was little more than the insertion of such phrases as "through the

Holy Spirit" as convenient into the decrees. More recently, under the influence of post–Vatican II theologians as well as the ecumenical dialogues, there has been a significant reclaiming of the central role of the Holy Spirit in the writings of Roman Catholic theologians and with this the uniting of the laying-on-of-hands as the preeminent ritual gesture that embodies that role.[11] In this regard, Godfrey Diekmann makes a telling observation. He writes:

> The restoration of the laying on of hands, besides centering attention on the Spirit, should also go far to eliminate our historically disastrous tendency to interpret the sacramental action in a mechanistic, impersonal fashion.[12]

This is an important reminder that our concern here is not ritual trivia, but rather the inner substance and meaning of what the rites signify.

---

11. Cf. John H. McKenna, *The Eucharistic Epiclesis* (Chicago: Hillenbrand Books, 2009), esp. 188–227.

12. Diekmann, "The Laying on of Hands," 350.

CHAPTER 7

Words of Consecration
–or Eucharistic Prayer?

T HE TITLE OF THIS CHAPTER is meant to raise a question of focus: where is the primary focus in the celebration of the Eucharist? And more particularly, where is the primary focus in the proclamation of the Great Thanksgiving, the Eucharistic Prayer? The Christological focus in Western theology that we noted in the previous chapter inevitably had significant influence upon the way the text of the Eucharistic Prayer was structured. Eventually this focus also influenced the development of the ritual actions that came to be required when the Prayer was said by a priest during the celebration of the Mass.

After the Western Church separated from the Orthodox East, the Roman Eucharistic Prayer took its definitive form without any explicit reference to the presence and action of the Holy Spirit. As we noted in the previous chapter, the Holy Spirit was referred to only in the context of doxological phrases addressed to the three Persons of the Holy Trinity. This difference of emphasis became one of the primary theological issues of conflict between East and West. For the Orthodox, the focus of the sacramental transformation of the gifts was identified with the action of the Holy Spirit. Yet even in this, as the focus intensified through the dispute with the Roman West, there was at least the suggestion of a "moment" when, as was taught in the West, "the eucharistic miracle" occurred. Certainly in the West, the rituals that developed within the Roman Canon at the recitation of the Words of Institution clearly embodied the idea of "a moment of consecration," and contributed to the theology and rituals that developed around it.

In Anglican writings on the Eucharist, there has been a consistent emphasis upon a holistic notion of the Prayer, namely that "it is the entire prayer which is consecratory."[1] Sometimes in Anglican practice, this claim has been obscured by ritual accretions taken over from other liturgical traditions, primarily from the Roman Rite. Given the origins of the English Church within the Western Roman tradition, it is not surprising that Anglican liturgical practice has been somewhat ambivalent on this question. The problem was given increased significance under the impact of the Catholic Revival of the nineteenth century.

As we observed earlier [chapter 4], the liturgical vacuum created by a general revulsion against "popery" within the English Church virtually eliminated ritual elements from Anglican practice. The Enlightenment dealt a death blow to any such ritual *hocus pocus*. The leaders of the Catholic Revival were thus faced with a serious problem: where in the reclamation of its Catholic roots could members of the English Church look for models of liturgical practice that might be adapted to the texts of the *Book of Common Prayer*?

It was particularly during the "second phase" of the Oxford Movement that this question became a serious concern. The early years of the Movement were not characterized by a particular concern for

---

1. This may be affirmed as well with regard to the Orthodox tradition. Cf. *Anglican-Orthodox Dialogue, The Dublin Statement 1984* (London: S.P.C.K., 1985), Appendix I, para. 30: "The consecration of the bread and wine results from the whole sacramental liturgy. . . . The deepest understanding of the hallowing of the elements rejects any theory of consecration by formula—whether by words of institution or *epiclesis*."

ritual matters, but rather about the recovery of traditional faith and practice. During those early years, it is likely that leaders such as Pusey and Newman would not have worn a stole in the celebration of the Holy Communion. Even the surplice was looked upon by some as "a popish rag."[2]

So where were Catholic models to be found? Various responses emerged in answer to this question. For some, the appropriate historical source for English liturgical practice was the medieval Latin Rite, that is, the Roman Rite as it had been celebrated in England. That rite had become almost universal in western Europe, although some historic local rites had been maintained as, for example, the Ambrosian Rite in Milan.

In England, however, the Roman Rite was in general use throughout the country, albeit celebrated with local ritual traditions known as a "Use." By the beginning of the sixteenth century there were at least five such "Uses" in England: Sarum (Salisbury), York, Hereford, Bangor, and Lincoln. For all of these, with regard to the texts, it was the Roman Rite that was celebrated, but with ritual variations according to a particular Use. Among the five mentioned above, the Sarum rite

---

2. Cf. *An Admonition to Parliament* (1572), written by two Puritan clergymen, had attacked the 1559 BCP of Elizabeth I for its inclusion of papish perversions. This suspicion concerning all Roman Catholic liturgical practices had continued in the more Protestant circles in England.

was the most influential.[3] The liturgical revisions undertaken by Archbishop Thomas Cranmer which led to the first *Book of Common Prayer* (1549) drew upon this Sarum heritage as a primary source. In his revisions of the Roman Eucharistic Prayer in the second BCP (1552), however, Cranmer accepted the emphasis of the continental reformers upon the Words of Institution as the biblical mandate for the eucharistic action. Thus the medieval emphasis upon the Words of Institution was maintained, but for a very different reason.

That Cranmer did away with the Roman ritual practices is not at all surprising: we see in this the influence of John Calvin who taught that Christians must worship God as God intends and not with human inventions of ceremonial. Hence all such ritual practices must be removed.[4] During the second phase of the Catholic Revival in the Church of England, however, these ritual practices were reclaimed based either upon their presence in the medieval Sarum Use, or on a simple return to the then-current ritual norms of the Roman Rite, viewing the Missal of Pius V (1570) (known since as "the Tridentine rite") as the appropriate model for a Catholic Eucharist.

This use of the then-current Roman Rite as a

---

3. Cf. G.J. Cuming, *A History of Anglican Liturgy,* 2nd ed. (London: Macmillan, 1982), 1–14.

4. "The Necessity of Reforming the Church" (1544), in *Selected Works of John Calvin* (Grand Rapids, MI: Baker Book House, 1983), 128.

source for Anglican liturgical practice took two forms: the first was the taking of the Roman ritual pattern and imposing it upon the text of Cranmer's Prayer in the form authorized in the 1662 *Book of Common Prayer*.[5] Others simply placed the Roman Missal on Anglican altars and used it, either in Latin or in English, in Anglican congregations.[6] The impact of this adoption of Roman ritual practices led to the resumption of the rituals connected to the "moment of consecration" theology, namely, elevations of the two Elements, genuflections, and the ringing of a bell. In imitation of Roman Catholic practice, it also led some clergy to adopt rather bizarre practices regarding posture and voice: in order to focus intently on the Words, the priest would bend forward, placing both elbows upon the altar, and say the Words in a different, more solemn tone of voice. To an observer of this action, it could appear that the priest was "talking to bread." In looking critically at what a presider *does* during the Prayer, we must be aware of what

5. The 1662 BCP continues to this day as the "official" book, although more recent supplementary books have appeared from the twentieth century to the present in the wake of demands for revision.

6. Needless to say, this solution was taken far less frequently: an Anglican priest using the Roman Rite is faced with a bizarre situation when he prays for the current pope as "our pope" while knowing that an earlier pope had declared Anglican ordinations to be invalid. This "Alice in Wonderland" situation can be found among a small number of clergy known as Anglo-papalists who hold that the break between Rome and Canterbury was a mistake and should, as much as possible, be ignored.

it is that the people *see*—what the ritual actions *say* to them.

To various degrees, this model has had widespread influence in Anglican ritual practice, even in parishes that would not be identified as Anglo-Catholic. While on a recent visit to the east coast to give a lecture, I attended the Eucharist at a parish I had not known before; nor did I know the rector. While the Eucharistic Prayer was being said, I was surprised by what the rector did. At the Words of Institution, there was a change of voice to a quieter and more dramatic tone; after the Words over the bread, the presider lifted the bread a couple of inches above the altar for a brief moment. This was followed by a deep bow. The same pattern was followed at the Words over the chalice. It was, in fact, the old Roman ritual modified.

This was for me a rather extreme example of "vestigial ritual." Given the theological 'shape' of the Eucharistic Prayers in the American BCP, and our heritage from the Non-Jurors with regard to the *epiclesis* of the Holy Spirit, what I saw that day was, to be frank, simply silly—and it looked silly. Our theology must affect what we do ritually.

Another ritual innovation taken up by some clergy during the last few decades is the lifting up of the right hand during the recitation of the Words over the bread, and then again in the Words over the chalice. I have seen this done on many occasions, and have wondered what the presider thinks that this gesture means. When I have inquired, the only response has been that the presider saw it done and decided to adopt it. This is a dangerous basis for ritual practice—unless one has a clear sense of why a gesture is being done.

I decided to try to learn where this particular gesture originated; the only source I have been able to find has the introduction of this practice in the mid-twentieth century by the late Canon Edward West at the Cathedral of St. John the Divine in New York City. The gesture as done by Canon West was not exactly what his imitators have taken up. When he presided at the Eucharist, and at the Words of Institution lifted his right hand, Canon West inserted the words of a Jewish blessing—a *berakah*—which he said in Hebrew in a low voice. In itself one might say that this was a rather charming inclusion of what was possibly an action of our Lord at the last supper. In the 1950s, this identification with the action of Jesus would not have been questioned since many people held the view that the presider was, in the Eucharistic Prayer, acting *in persona Christi*, in the person of Christ.

Further reflection on the role of the presider in the decades since that time has led us to look at this ministry in a different way. For one thing, liturgical scholarship has reminded us that the earliest title for a bishop (or priest) presiding at a Eucharist was to understand this action as *in persona ecclesiae*, in the person of the Church.[7] Many of us can remember the rubrics in the 1928 prayer book, which instructed the priest to take the bread and wine into his hands as an embodiment of the references in the Prayer to Jesus's taking of the bread and the cup during that final meal with the disciples. This strong identification of the presider with Jesus must be questioned given our gradual recovery of a sense of the entire community being the "celebrants" of the Eucharist and the primary role of the presider as being the voice of the Church expressed through the sacramental ministry of the ordained person.

We should remember that the identification of a strictly *male* priesthood with Jesus has been given as one of the reasons why women might not be ordained: the objection was that, being female, they could not "take the role of Jesus" in the Eucharistic Prayer. The lifting up of the right hand must be seen within the perspective of this issue: a priest at the altar is not imitating Jesus at the last supper, but is presiding at an action in which the gathered people of God are full participants.

---

7. Cf. Gerard Austin, O.P., "In Persona Christi at the Eucharist," in *Eucharist: Toward the Third Millennium*, Gerard Austin et al., eds. (Chicago: Liturgical Training Publications, 1997), 81–86.

This understanding must have an influence upon the rituals that a presider employs.

What I have encountered with many clergy is a vague sense that the priest "must do something" at this point. But "something" is being done: the Eucharistic Prayer, the Great Thanksgiving, is being proclaimed, and in our theological tradition, as was true in the early centuries of Christianity, consecration is effected by the entire Prayer, not through a manipulation of the bread and wine. Bread and wine are placed on the altar; the Prayer is proclaimed over the designated gifts; and then the Presence of Christ is ritually acknowledged, perhaps with a profound bow in silence, or perhaps a genuflection. "Consecration by manipulation," as I was told by an English monk, "is a thing of the past."

If an elevation of the gifts has a place in the Eucharistic Prayer, then it would occur at the doxology, the original point at which a lifting up of the consecrated Bread and Wine took place. This lifting of the Elements at that time is the source of the word *anaphora*. What is not appropriate at this point is the elaborate pattern of signs of the cross, which developed late in the Roman Catholic ritual, known as "the baroque flourish." When the priest's back was toward the people, this gesture could not be seen by the congregation, but when the presider is facing the people, this gesture is at the very least distracting and confusing, the worst aspect being the use of the consecrated Bread as a kind of talisman with which one makes the sign of the cross. The Bread is to be eaten, not played with.[8]

The Issue for the American Rite

From what has been said above, it is evident that any rituals attached to the Words of Institution raise a particular question for the ritual practices followed by the clergy of the Episcopal Church. From the first American prayer book of 1789 until the present book of 1979, the incorporation of an *epiclesis*, an Oblation, and the memorial *anamnesis* has been normative. This theological model for the Eucharistic Prayer in the American prayer book tradition originated in the Church at Antioch. This pattern is based upon the most frequently celebrated Eucharistic Prayer of the Byzantine Rite.[9]

The one exception to this is Prayer C in the *Book of Common Prayer* (1979). This prayer was drafted by the late Howard Galley, and in it he chose to split the *epiclesis* in a pattern currently used in

---

8. Joseph A. Jungmann, *The Mass of the Roman Rite: Its Origins and Development* (New York: Benziger Brothers, 1955), 259–74.

9. This prayer is known as the Antiochene Anaphora of St. John Chrysostom. Cf. Hugh Wybrew, " The Byzantine Liturgy from the *Apostolic Constitutions* to the Present Day," in Cheslyn Jones et al., eds., *The Study of Liturgy,* revised ed. (New York: Oxford University Press, 1992), 252–63.

the Eucharistic Prayers of the Roman Rite. A split *epiclesis* is a form in which, prior to the Words of Institution, there is an invocation of the Holy Spirit to consecrate the gifts. The second *epiclesis* comes after the Institution Narrative and the *anamnesis/* Oblation; its focus is upon the Communion of the faithful. This pattern is found in an early form that originated in Egypt,[10] and it is the pattern taken up in the post–Vatican II liturgical reforms because it is understood to focus the consecration itself in the Words of Institution that follow the first *epiclesis.*

It was the opinion of Howard Galley that Episcopalians should be aware that the Invocation of the Holy Spirit could be expressed in a form other than that in all previous American prayer books. One might perhaps defend this as a "teaching device," but among liturgical scholars it has been viewed quite negatively since it sacrifices the theological complementarity of the two dimensions of the Spirit's action in the Eucharist. The current prayer book of the Anglican Church of Canada includes Galley's text, but with several important modifications, including the uniting of the two dimensions of the Spirit's action in a single *epiclesis,* which follows the Institution Narrative.[11] Other adapta-

---

10. Cf. E.J. Yarnold, S.J., "The Egyptian Type," in his article "The Liturgy of the Faithful in the Fourth and Early Fifth Centuries," in *The Study of Liturgy,* 237–39.

11. See Eucharistic Prayer 4 in *The Book of Alternative Service of the Anglican Church of Canada* (Toronto: Anglican Book Centre, 1985), 201–03.

tions of Galley's prayer have been used at various liturgical occasions in the United States as well, also with the unity of the *epiclesis* restored, so it is likely that some people are at least aware that there is a theological issue being raised by its 1979 form.

This question of the form of the *epiclesis* is directly connected with the question of whether the medieval pattern of rituals that developed around the Words of Institution can be justified in current practice. Even asking the question can surprise some (clergy as well as laity), since most of us are accustomed to the presider "doing *something*" in the course of proclaiming the Prayer. Ritual practices have an extraordinary tenacity, and within the eucharistic action those practices can take on a remarkable significance for the piety of clergy and laity alike. What we have done or seen done over a period of years becomes for us a normative expectation, so that if it is not done, we can feel that something is wrong or missing.

In discussing this question with both bishops and priests, it is clear to me that frequently a ritual pattern learned at the time of ordination has been preserved without any further critical reflection, performed, in a sense, by rote. Whatever form that ritual pattern has taken during many years of sacramental ministry, it becomes firmly embedded in personal piety, and questioning it can be experienced as a threat to that piety.

The question being posed here is one which Anglican liturgical scholars have been raising for a century. In 1913 Vernon Staley made this observation:

> It cannot be said too emphatically
> that the words "This is my body"—
> "This is my blood," were not our
> Lord's words of *Consecration*, but His
> words of *Administration*. His words of
> administration, it is true, declare the
> effect of His previous consecration,
> but we cannot by any ingenuity twist
> them to become His actual words of
> consecration.[12]

And so the question we must face with regard to ritual actions in the Eucharistic Prayer is: what is it that *consecrates* the bread and wine to be for us the sacrament of Christ's Body and Blood? The consensus among sacramental theologians would suggest that consecration is better understood to be by thanksgiving rather than by a moment or formula of consecration. This reminds us that the consecration of the gifts is itself composed of three primary aspects: thanksgiving to God the Father, the memorial (*anamnesis*) of God the Son, and

---

12. Vernon Staley, *The Manual Acts*, Alcuin Club Prayer Book Revision Pamphlets IV (London: Mowbrays, 1913), 17.

the invocation (*epiclesis*) of God the Holy Spirit. The consecration is effected in the context of a Trinitarian confession of faith.

There is another important factor to be brought into this discussion of the role taken by the Words of Institution: what if these words are not in the Prayer at all? In an important article published some forty years ago, John Austin Baker wrote, with regard to the content of the Eucharistic Prayer:

> We are not obliged to use the
> institution narrative or the words;
> and if we do, they supply us only with
> a narrative reminder of the reason
> why our central act of worship takes
> the form it does, the action around
> and over bread and wine. These
> physical data are the only things to
> which we are tied, the medium of our
> *anamnesis*.[13]

We observed earlier that for many decades Anglican writers have affirmed that the entire Prayer is "consecratory." If so, then certain implications emerge, among them that a Eucharistic Prayer might not of necessity include the reported words of Jesus at that final supper with his disciples.

This is probably the most surprising question

---

13. John Austin Baker, "The 'Institution' Narratives and the Christian Eucharist," in *Thinking about the Eucharist*, papers by members of the Church of England Doctrine Commission (London: SCM Press, 1972), 56.

that could be posed concerning the consecration of the gifts, and it is one that quite recently has been raised among Roman Catholics. A primitive Eucharistic Prayer known as the Anaphora of Addai and Mari has been in continuous use by Assyrian Christians since very early times.[14] That primitive prayer does not include the words of Jesus over the bread and cup. Within the context of an ecumenical dialogue seeking reconciliation between Rome and the Eastern Assyrian Church, three Roman Congregations and Pope John Paul II affirmed that Addai and Mari is a valid form of Eucharistic Prayer.[15]

The possibility of there being no Institution Narrative was also raised by the distinguished Anglican liturgical historian, the late Geoffrey Cuming. In an article published almost thirty years ago, Cuming based his observations on the work of Louis Ligier on four very early Prayers marked by an "extreme brevity and simplicity."[16] These prayers contain no Words of Institution. If a Eucharistic Prayer included no Words of Institution, it is obvious that these Words could *not* have been understood as the *moment* or formula of consecration.

---

14. Some scholars suggest that it may have originated as early as the third century in Edessa.

15. See the article by Robert F. Taft, S.J., "Mass Without the Consecration?" in *America* 188 (16), May 12, 2003, 7–11.

16. Geoffrey Cuming, "Forum: Four Very Early Anaphoras," *Worship* (58 (2), March 1984, 168–72. Cf. Louis Ligier, "The Origins of the Eucharistic Prayer," *Studia Liturgica* 9 (1973), 9.

Whether we refer either to the Eucharistic Prayer written by Archbishop Cranmer or to the Roman Canon, which the Reformers generally condemned, we have for centuries been accustomed to hearing a very long prayer over the bread and wine. This model seems to have emerged in the fourth century's rhetorical style of proclamation. This was a context in which the role of the presider gradually became so dominant that all the constitutive elements of the rite had to be brought together in his role as the proclaimer of this Great Thanksgiving.

The implications of this discussion lead us to suggest that once the bread and wine have been placed upon the altar, the posture of the presider is simply that of the arms extended in prayer, the posture known as the *orans*. The earliest gesture, which seems to have come into use during the Eucharistic Prayer, is the "laying on of hands" upon the gifts, traditionally associated with the *epiclesis*. This is the primary manual action in the Prayer, as it is in all sacramental rites. The presider does not "confect the sacrament," but rather proclaims the Church's prayer over the gifts of bread and wine which, through the Holy Spirit's action, become for us the Body and Blood of the Lord.

There is yet one more related question regarding the Words of Institution that must not be overlooked, and that is the rubrical direction that has been present in all editions of the *Book of Common Prayer* since that of 1662: the requirement that the presider touch both elements at the time of the Institution Narrative. In the 1549 BCP, Archbishop Cranmer removed all other ceremonies from this point in the medieval ritual, retaining only that the priest should touch each element at the Words. Massey Shepherd suggests that even this simplified act was associated in the minds of the clergy with the medieval pattern, and thus from 1552 onward there was no authorization for any "manual acts." The 1662 BCP, however, restored the touching of the elements with expanded directions. Shepherd sees this as based upon two factors:

> First, symbolical, to imitate the
> actions of our Lord at the Last Supper;
> and secondly, practical, to break the
> bread in preparation for the people's
> Communion, which, in the English rite,
> comes immediately after these words.[17]

Although this explanation is appropriate for the period in which it was written, we must now look at both these reasons with a critical eye. First, the suggestion that the priest during the Eucharistic Prayer is "imitating the actions of our Lord" has been firmly rejected by theologians and liturgical

---

17. Massey Hamilton Shepherd, Jr., *The Oxford American Prayer Book Commentary* (New York: Oxford University Press, 1950), 80.

scholars. Even if interpreted as supplying the biblical warrant for the action, the idea itself that the presider is acting *in persona Christi* does not survive a critical consideration of the role of the presider in early eucharistic practice. As was noted earlier, the actions of the presider are done *in persona ecclesiae*: the priest acts as an ordained member of the community, as a member of the Body of Christ and not as Christ himself.

The second factor noted by Dr. Shepherd for the inclusion of the touching is that the rubric indicates not only a touching, but also that the bread is broken at that moment. In the 1979 BCP, the rubric about touching the elements has been retained, but *not* the indication that the bread should be broken at that point. The reason for this is, quite simply, that the historic and independent place of the Fraction Rite has been recovered in the 1979 book. This is a further confirmation, based upon ancient practice, that the priest is not imitating the presumed actions of Jesus at the Last Supper.

Yet the fact remains that the requirement that the priest touch the bread and the cup (and any other vessels) is still operative, and as a priest of the Church, this is what I do when I preside. There are, however, reactions to this that are beginning to emerge along with an expanding awareness that for many centuries, the presider did not *do* anything during the Eucharistic Prayer except to proclaim it. In the Church of England, this option appeared in *The Alternative Service Book 1980* in a note appended to "The Order for Holy Communion" which permits "traditional manual acts" to be used by the presider "[i]n addition to the taking of the bread and the cup" which is done when the elements are placed upon the altar. In other words, such manual acts are permitted but are optional.[18] In the American Church, this development was noted by the late Marion Hatchett in an important essay dealing with the "unfinished business" remaining with regard to the 1979 BCP. Hatchett notes that most of the more recent revisions of Anglican prayer books "have dropped the requirement of Manual Acts during the reading of the Institution Narrative." Hatchett affirms this development when he notes that "Even the restrained use of Manual Acts that is required in the Eucharistic Prayers of BCP 79 tends to signify that the Institution Narrative is a moment of consecration."[19]

This question was first brought home to me in my experience while on retreat with the Anglican community of Benedictine nuns at West Malling, near Canterbury, where for many years a Eucharistic

---

18. *The Alternative Service Book 1980* (Cambridge, UK: Cambridge University Press, 1980), 117n.16.

19. "Unfinished Business in Prayer Book Revision," *Leaps and Boundaries. The Prayer Book in the 21st century*, ed. Paul V. Marshall and Lesley Northup (Harrisburg, PA: Morehouse Publishing, 1997), 28.

Prayer developed within the community has been used in which the presider does not touch the elements during the prayer. It was written by a patristic scholar in the community and is based upon her research of early patterns of the Prayer.

I have presided at this rite countless times. Once I have placed the bread and wine on the altar, I lift my hands to sing the *Sursum corda* and do not lower them until the Prayer ends with a doxological hymn sung by the community. Thus I have learned through my own experience the extraordinary theological integrity of this pattern of eucharistic praise with no manual acts, and yet with a clear understanding of the consecration of the gifts in a common act of thanksgiving. *Doing* nothing, yet doing everything.

CHAPTER 8

Ritual Integrity

T HE WORD 'BLEEDING' ENTERED MY liturgical vocabulary spontaneously. It happened one day in class when I was discussing various pastoral matters that had been raised in the transition from the 1928 *Book of Common Prayer* to that of 1979, and particularly the impact of this transition on the liturgical practices of parish priests. It is in this context that I use the term 'bleeding'—when a presider's ritual pattern practiced in one liturgical context flows over—bleeds—into a different ritual context with a different set of liturgical, theological, and ritual concerns.

The question was raised for me during the early 1980s when the Episcopal Church was still passing through a time of transition to the then "new" *Book of Common Prayer*. As one worshipping in the pews, it dawned upon me that apart from the texts, the liturgical patterns I observed were identical to those appropriate to the eucharistic texts of the 1928 prayer book. This tended to be true both in Anglo-Catholic and "low church" parishes. In spite of the use of the new Rite II, everything else was exactly as it had been. Many parishes had made the transition to the 1979 BCP with regard to the liturgical texts, but had made no changes with regard to the ritual. This may have been a pastoral tactic to fend off negative reactions from the members of the parish whose liturgical expectations had been fully—and firmly—formed by the 1928 book. I suspect that there were no ritual changes because those practices were deeply planted within the piety of the clergy. The problem with this, however, was that the transition from the 1928 BCP to the 1979 book cut much deeper than changes in the texts. A reevaluation of theology as well as liturgical performance patterns was now required, and this was a disturbing task to undertake.

Earlier revisions of the American prayer book had, by comparison, been rather modest: some changes of wording, some additions of new forms of prayer, and occasionally some ritual adjustments. But in the 1979 *Book of Common Prayer*, a more profound revision had taken place. The former

dominant role of the clergy in the various rites
had been based upon the assumption by clergy
and laity alike that the liturgy was essentially the
action of the clergy in which the laity participated
by listening and observing. This view had shaped
the expectations of both groups. Although this
understanding was more officially embraced by the
Roman Church, we must admit that for Anglicans
as well, most liturgical rites were said by the
clergy, and more specifically by the "celebrant." It
was not at all uncommon for the celebrant not only
to preside and to proclaim the Eucharistic Prayer,
but also to read the appointed epistle and gospel.

The clergy and laity who were given the responsibility of developing the rites that would eventually be included in the 1979 book did not see their
task as a modest revision. Important developments in the general life of the Church had begun
to shape a different understanding of the liturgy:
all members of the Church were, by their Baptism,
viewed as full participants in its ministries, with
ordination being the designation of some members
of the community for specific liturgical and sacramental roles. The word 'ministry' itself had come to
be understood as embracing a wide range of forms
of service, among which liturgical ministry played
one—albeit important—part.

For many clergy, however, the struggle was not
only to become familiar with the new texts of the

1979 rites, but the far more difficult task of understanding those rites as "the work of the people"—which is what the root of the word *liturgy* denotes. In this perspective, the liturgy is the common prayer of the whole people of God assembled for worship. Thus, a new understanding of what we might call "the body language" of the priest presiding at the corporate prayer-action of the entire assembly was necessary. Again, this is the challenge I have named as 'bleeding'—body language and performance practices reflective of an older style of presidency bleeding into a rite where they are theologically an anomaly.

This response is not at all surprising since liturgical ritual practice operates at a deeply personal level. The previous model may be associated with years of experience and fond memories, forming an unexamined expectation about what a priest *does* at the altar during the Eucharistic Prayer. This personal, emotional response is as likely of lay members of a community as of the ordained. The rector of a parish here in California told me recently of a remark made by a member of the parish concerning the way in which a much older, retired priest presided: she said that "his Mass is holier." And when the rector inquired as to what this meant, the parishioner said, "He makes so many signs of the cross."

In my own ministry as a newly ordained priest

in the Diocese of Puerto Rico, I learned that often members of a parish will attach great significance to gestures I knew to be of minor importance. We need to take their perspective very seriously: it tells us what the laity are *seeing* during the course of the liturgy, and how what they see shapes what is significant for their personal piety.

Clergy may follow a particular ritual pattern for years with personal reasons for what they do, but no awareness of how those actions are perceived and understood by the people in the pew. If communicants become attached to certain gestures but lack a sense of what the Eucharist means in the context of the Christian life, then presiders must ask themselves if their manner of presiding is sending the wrong signals.

Liturgical experience is unquestionably formative: it shapes an understanding of the meaning of a rite. But if what is formed is, as it were, skewed, then a spiritually healthy formation cannot take place. And if filters are operating which the parish priest does not take into account, then there is important work to be done by all involved. The significance of liturgical catechesis must not be underestimated.

I have often been told by former Baptists that they became Episcopalians because of the beauty of our liturgy. That is, in fact, a very important aspect of liturgical worship, but the liturgy must be based upon more than an aesthetic attraction, which can remain superficial to the depth of the liturgical experience. This means that, especially in our culture, pre-liturgical priorities—catechesis and the development of a common liturgical (symbolic) language—must be attended to, and the 'bleeding' of former pieties must be addressed.

Liturgical 'bleeding' may be most clearly appreciated in the making of the sign of the cross at various points in the liturgy. Why is the sign of the cross made in three specific points of the liturgy, most particularly? Two of these are parallel: the making of the sign at the end of the *Gloria in excelsis* (Glory to God in the highest) and at the end of the Creed. None of the books on the history of the Eucharist explains why the cross was inserted into the rite at those two points. As I have reflected on this, a theory has emerged for me which, of course, cannot be proven because it seems to have been taken up by the laity through a misunderstanding of what the priest was doing at the altar.

In England during the later Middle Ages, the custom developed in some places that before the presider sang "The Lord be with you," he would make the sign of the cross before turning to the people. Since the Collect of the Day immediately followed the *Gloria in excelsis*, this meant that the priest made the sign at the end of the *Gloria* and that what the people *saw* was a cross not as visually prior to the Salutation but as a concluding gesture to the singing of the *Gloria*. This is another example of liturgical bleeding—from one context into another.

The sign of the cross at the end of the Creed follows the same pattern: in the medieval rite, immediately after the Creed there was a Collect, which had originally been part of the Prayers of the People when they had in the early centuries taken place at that point. In the fifth century, this intercessory rite had been absorbed into the recitation of the Eucharistic Prayer, but the vestigial Salutation had remained. As with the *Gloria in excelsis*, the priest made the sign of the cross before singing the Salutation, but what the people saw was the sign done at the end of the Creed. I have been unable to find any other explanation for the sign being made at those two points.

A somewhat different example is found with the sign of the cross at the words of the *Benedictus quit venit*—"Blessed is he who comes in the name of the Lord." We have evidence that already in the seventh century, the Eucharistic Prayer had, because of its sacred character, come to be said in a voice so low as to be inaudible to the people. In the medieval sung Mass, it became common practice that the choir would stop singing after the *Sanctus*, so that the people might look up and adore at the two elevations of the Elements; the choir would then continue with the singing of the *Benedictus qui venit.* But a pious custom had developed of making the sign of the cross as each Element was lifted up, so that the sign at the elevation of the chalice occurred as the choir resumed singing the *Benedictus.* These are good examples of how gestures become attached to moments in the liturgy which, if this suggestion is correct, originated in a different context. Thus we see that in the evolution of the liturgy, gestures have sometimes taken on a life of their own and are then performed as a kind of automatic drill often with increased frequency.

It is not that symbolic gestures require explanation: that is not the way we claim their meaning in any case. But a symbol must be "entered into"—and that requires a certain orientation about how those symbols work.[1] Often both clergy and laity become attached in their personal piety to practices of secondary importance on the surface of a rite while overlooking the primary symbol—the meaning of the rite itself. One may hear a person say, "That is merely a symbol"—yet this phrase itself is an indi-

---

1. Symbols are multivalent, that is, they embody many levels of meaning. This can make engagement with a symbol very difficult for a certain mind-set in which a meaning is seen only in the literal sense of a symbol. This literalism is characteristic of some forms of American religion, and, of course, it undermines the nature of a sacred symbol in which, in the traditional understanding, "the outward sign" is distinguished from "the inward and spiritual grace." A symbol that 'works' does not require explanation because the outward sign embodies the inward meaning while yet being distinct from it.

cation that what a symbol *is* has not been understood. It was my great privilege many years ago to take a course with Paul Tillich, and one day his focus in class was on the meaning of 'symbol'. At one point he said to us with great passion, "Never say 'merely a symbol.'" Tillich's passion on this was quite justified for if the members of a liturgical church do not understand the nature of symbols, the essential sense of their liturgical prayer is undermined.

The problem may be that Anglicans have, as it were, lived off our liturgical heritage without adequately mining the depth of its meaning, the ways in which it embodies for us our encounter with the Holy One. This has often left some members who are regular and faithful in their attendance at the liturgy nevertheless worshiping on the surface of the symbols without drinking from the life-giving waters that spring from their depth.

Words Mean What They Say

In the liturgical rites of the *Book of Common Prayer*, we find in certain texts or rubrics indications of the rite's underlying sense, which, if ignored, can contradict the theological or ritual dimensions of the rite itself. One example is found in regard to the roles of the ordained liturgical ministers, specifically in the use of the word "deacon." This word is often used as an indication of a function or set of functions that a person—any person—may perform.

Yet the word "deacon" is not merely a functional designation: it is the name of an Order among the Church's ordained ministries. We should note that in both the Orthodox and Roman liturgical traditions, a bishop or priest is *forbidden* to vest as a deacon. The issue here is one of ministerial integrity and not simply "playing a role." We need to consider seriously the reasons why our sister churches with whom we share the threefold ministerial model of bishop, priest, and deacon take such a strongly negative position on this question.

I remember a major liturgical celebration soon after I became a member of the Episcopal Church during my college years. There were three "sacred ministers" at the altar: celebrant, deacon, and sub-deacon. The choreography of the three ministers indicated that this was seen as an important ritual event. The problem, however, which I came to understand only years later, was that all three of the ministers were, in fact, priests. Eventually I came to realize that this practice embodied an erosion of the integrity of the authentic diaconate, viewed then as "an inferior Office" in the ordination rite of a deacon in the 1928 *Book of Common Prayer*.[2]

---

2. Cf. 1928 BCP, 535

Further, with regard to the Anglican tradition regarding ordination rites, there is the historical fact that in his revision of the rites, Archbishop Thomas Cranmer abolished the sub-diaconate as a "minor order" at the same time that he recovered the patristic sense of the "major orders" of bishop, priest, and deacon. This marked a rejection of the medieval teaching that a bishop is a priest (then viewed as the primary Order of ministry because of his authority to celebrate the Mass), but a priest who has pastoral jurisdiction over a diocese, including the authority to ordain. Cranmer's ordination rites were a bold step toward the recovery of the early model of the episcopate which understood the bishop as the source of ordained ministry.[3] In Cranmer's model, parish priests are seen as an extension of the bishop's ministry, serving as the pastoral and sacramental leaders of local communities within the diocese.

Thus, in current liturgical practice, our theology of Holy Orders would suggest that if a priest is assisting a presider when no deacon is present, that priest should not be called "the deacon" but rather an "assisting priest." That is what they *are*—so that is what they should be called.[4] If a

---

3. It was only in the twentieth century that Pope Pius XII recovered this pattern for the Roman Church.

4. Cf. Kevin Flynn, "Once a Deacon . . .?" in D.R. Holeton, ed., *Anglican Orders and Ordinations* (Cambridge, UK: Grove Books, 1997), 41–45.

deacon is present, of course, it is their prerogative to fulfill the traditional diaconal ministries.

Yet another example of the imperative that our liturgical practices be in accord with what the rites actually indicate is found in the musical aspect of the celebration, especially with regard to what is usually called "the Ordinary of the Mass."[5] The question I am raising here is concerned with items that should normatively be sung.

In the evolution of liturgical practice in the Western Church, the sung dimension of the rites was lost when, for a variety of reasons, a rite was said rather than sung. This shift may have been based upon a common sense adjustment when weekday services increased in frequency, often attended by a smaller gathering of people with limited musical resources. The emergence of the "said liturgy" led to the anomaly that texts that were intended for singing might be said instead. The *Gloria in excelsis* is an important example of this since the text is clearly a hymn, the hymn of the angels at the birth of Jesus.[6] Thus, although commonly included at a weekday celebration of the feast of a saint, this text would often be said rather than sung.

We have become so accustomed to this 'adjustment'

---

5. The Ordinary is made up of certain standard texts of the eucharistic rite, namely, the *Kyrie eleison,* the *Gloria in excelsis,* the Creed, the *Sanctus,* and the *Agnus Dei.*

6. Luke 2:14.

that we often overlook the fact that this is indicated in the prayer book as a second option. In both Rite I and Rite II, the rubric at this point is important: *"When appointed, the following hymn or some other song of praise is sung or said."*[7] Significant norms are indicated by this rubric: first, that this text is not used at all celebrations of the Eucharist but *"when appointed."* This reminds us that the *Gloria in excelsis* is normally used on Sundays, the weekly feast of the Lord's resurrection, or at the celebration of the commemoration of a saint. The phrase "is sung or said" reminds us that, in the 'language of rubrics,' what is indicated first (i.e., *sung*) is the preferred option. Finally, this rubric also gives an option: *or some other song of praise*. This means that some other appropriate hymn may be sung as an alternative—but again, normally a hymn is *sung*.

This latter point is simply ritual common sense, namely, that a hymn text is normally sung. We never *say* the text of "The Star-Spangled Banner": we understand that it is a hymn without our being reminded—and so we sing it, even if we cannot sing it well. There is no reason why this same common sense should not apply to hymn texts in the liturgy. Whereas the various sung versions of the *Gloria in excelsis* are often difficult for a congregation, especially a small one with limited musical resources,

7. BCP, 324, 356.

there are numerous simple hymns of praise that can fulfill that expectation.

If it appears that I am making a mountain out of a molehill, I believe that this example points to a much more fundamental and significant issue: are liturgical texts simply words on a page without any relation to reality?—or are they in accord with the sense of the rite itself? Do our practices embody something *real*? If not, then should we be doing them at all?

Misguided Emphasis

Often, liturgical ministers feel they must add words to the prayer book texts, perhaps to give additional emphasis. This can, although done with the best of intentions, produce some unfortunate theological consequences. Two particular examples come to mind from my own experience. The first has to do with a deacon's reading of the Gospel.

At the conclusion of the reading, the prayer book indicates that the deacon (or an assisting priest) will say, "The Gospel of the Lord," to which the people respond, "Praise to you, Lord Christ." Yet on many occasions I have heard the acclamation said, "This is the Gospel of the Lord." I suspect that the ministers who do this see it as an emphasis, but the implications are far more serious than that. When the Gospel book is lifted up at that point, as is often done, the added "this" suggests a reference to the book, in which case it is quite inappropriate: "this" is not "the Gospel of the Lord;" "this" is the book of the Gospels. There is an important distinction. The Gospel is heard in and through its proclamation—it is the Word announced in the hearing of God's people gathered. This well-intentioned addition in fact puts the emphasis in the wrong place. When the rite was being drafted in the mid-1970s, the understanding of those who prepared the text was that the phrase "The Gospel of the Lord" is an acclamation of the Gospel that had just been proclaimed. The people who prepared the rite really did know what they were doing.

Another example of inappropriate emphasis has to do with the giving of Communion. On some occasions when I have been standing with my hands extended to receive the consecrated Bread, the minister has placed it on my hand and said, "This is the Body Christ, the bread of heaven." Again, this is theologically misleading and indicates an inadequate theology of the Real Presence of our Lord. "The Body of Christ" is an acclamation of the Christ present to us in the entirety of the eucharistic rite: yes, present to us in the eucharistic Gifts at Communion, but also present to us in the proclamation of the Word through the reading of Scripture and in the preaching; present to us in the assembly of God's people and in our common prayer; and present to us through the ministry of the ordained members of the community.[8] Adding the word "this" unintentionally narrows our discernment of the Presence of Christ and isolates that Presence in the consecrated gifts. We need to hear again the words of Saint Augustine to his people at Hippo: "You are the bread on the altar; behold your mystery."[9] The consecrated gifts are to us as a mirror, the Body of Christ as mirror to the Body of Christ. If we do not see Christ in the people around us, we cannot claim to see him in the consecrated gifts.

The Doxology and the Fraction

There are two dramatic ritual actions at the conclusion of the Eucharistic Prayer and at the Fraction that require attention.

1. The Eucharistic Prayer is the primary prayer of the entire celebration—it is the heart of the eucharistic action, and, as we observed in the previous chapter, the gifts are appropriately lifted up at the conclusion of the Prayer rather than at the Words of Institution. This is the moment when the entire assembly of the people affirms the Prayer and the action of

---

8. One of the most important insights in this regard came from the Roman Catholic bishops at the Second Vatican Council. In the *Constitution on the Sacred Liturgy*, it was taught that there are many modes in which Christ is present in the Church; cf. *Sacrosacntum Concilium* (December 4, 1963), para. 7.

9. St. Augustine, Sermon 272 (c. 405 AD). Daniel J. Sheerin, *The Eucharist* (Wilmington, DE: Michael Glazier, 1986), 94–96.

the presider with their "Amen." St. Ambrose spoke of this Amen, the most significant of the entire rite, as "sounding like thunder." In other words, this is a primary focus within the entire eucharistic action. For that reason, this conclusion to the Prayer requires careful thought.

Often a presider may stop saying the text immediately prior to the words of the doxology, hand a chalice to the deacon or an assisting priest, then pick up the bread or a paten holding the bread—and finally resume the singing (or saying) of the words. This interruption is strange to hear and to observe: it interrupts the sense and flow of the text needlessly. If the presider wants the deacon (or assistant) to lift up the chalice, which is certainly appropriate, is it not possible for the "choreography" of this action to be planned in such a way that the flow of the Prayer and its internal sense are respected?

When the presider prefers to lift up both elements, perhaps because there is no assistant or simply as a way of maintaining the flow of the Prayer, the use of various types of bread can create a different problem. This is not in any way a negative reaction to the use of other types of bread: the bread of the Eucharist should be real bread, and the use of wafers raises questions of credibility.[10] If another type of bread is used, however, the presider must take into account the impact of that upon the concluding ritual.

Many of us have seen an unleavened host suspended over a chalice during the doxology. Images of this are often used as iconic representations of the Eucharist itself. But this gesture of placing the bread above the chalice for the final elevation does not work—or is made far more problematic—when ordinary types of bread are used. Yet I have seen the action performed by presiders, who have somehow accepted the idea that during the doxology the bread should be held above the chalice without any understanding of its historical or liturgical origins. It is at moments like this that the presider's personal piety and intention can clash with the visual reality for a congregation. If the lifting up of the consecrated Gifts is done only by the presider, one hand can lift the paten and with the other the chalice without an interruption to the flow of the Prayer. The presider may not be aware that holding a loaf of bread above a chalice is visually dissonant if not ludicrous—but that is what the people see.

10. Aidan Kavanagh once commented that at his first reception of Communion, he could believe that the little host was the Body of Christ, . . . but bread?

2. A few moments after the Eucharistic Prayer has concluded and the Lord's Prayer has been said, the Fraction Rite—"The Breaking of the Bread"—takes place. This rite takes its name from a biblical reference to the supper on the evening of the Resurrection. In the Gospel of Luke, at the end of the report of the encounter at Emmaus, we hear these words about the apostles who had returned from sharing a table with the Lord: "he had been made known to them in the breaking of the bread."[11]

This rite has been recovered in its integrity in both Rites I and II in the 1979 *Book of Common Prayer.*[12] It is important to note the rubrical directions at this point in the rite and to understand their sense. The first rubric states that *"The Celebrant breaks the consecrated Bread"* and the second that *"A period of silence is kept."* The second rubric is integral to the first and is not optional. Frequently, however, the second rubric is not observed. In fact, on many occasions, I have heard the words "Christ our Passover is sacrificed for us" sung or said at the same moment that the fraction takes place. At one parish I visited, the presider lifted the bread high above his head, although the altar was facing

11. Luke 24:35.
12. Cf. BCP, 337, 364.

the people, and audibly *cracked* the bread exactly at the word "sacrificed."

Perhaps this was intended as a dramatic ritual moment, but it revealed a complete misunderstanding of both the rubrics and the text. The rubric that *"silence is kept"* is quite intentional and supports the meaning of the rite itself. To break the bread at the word "sacrificed"—although perhaps the presider did not intend this—mis-identifies the "breaking of the bread" solely with the death of Christ on the cross. The essential sense of the fraction is for the sharing of the broken bread in Communion. This is the reason why the drafters of the rite specifically asked for silence after the fraction: *silence*—awe—is the appropriate response to our knowing Christ in the breaking of the bread. The text that follows the silence is an acclamation of the whole Paschal Mystery: what it evokes is not only the death on the cross, but the entire paschal event of the death and resurrection of Jesus.

There is thus a twofold aspect to this rite: first, bread is broken to be shared, and second, to symbolize the unity of the Church as the one bread is shared in Communion. Obviously this meaning is most evident when a single loaf is used. But even if the number of communicants requires the use of more than one loaf, the breaking of one loaf at this point in the liturgy implies that it will be shared. The use of individual unleavened wafers does not support that meaning. Even the so-called "priest's host"—the larger wafer which can be broken and shared—is often consumed by the presider alone.

It is also as a symbol of unity that the *Additional Directions* that follow the eucharistic rites indicate that "During the Great Thanksgiving, it is appropriate that there be only one chalice on the Altar, and, if need be, a flagon of wine from which additional chalices may be filled after the Breaking of the Bread."[13] This reminds us that a fundamental symbol—in this case, the one chalice reflective of the unity of God's people—should not be obscured on the basis of utility.

The Sense and Value of Rubrics

Our discussion of the rubrics in the Fraction Rite suggests the need for fuller attention to the role of rubrics in liturgical celebrations. For this, I must begin with an affirmation: I am not a rubrical fundamentalist. There are contexts in which the pastoral judgment of a priest justifies a liturgical adjustment based upon common sense in a particular situation. A practical parallel to this may

---

13. BCP, 407.

be seen with regard to traffic lights. Generally we know that when we see a red light, we need to stop, and that if we continue driving, a collision may occur. But if we arrive at a traffic light and an officer is standing there who indicates that, in spite of a red light, we should continue driving, we also know that the presence of the officer indicates some unusual situation exists which requires that the normal observance of the red light be ignored.

This may be a rather 'homey' metaphor, but I think it makes the point with regard to the role of rubrics: they offer to presiders and officiants basic ritual guidelines for normal situations. In the liturgical tradition of the prayer book, rubrics have tended to be general and minimal, quite unlike the medieval ritual documents that spelled out in minute detail every action that a priest was *required* to do.

Attitudes toward rubrics range rather widely. I was once told that "if a single asterisk is removed" (as our musician had done in a musical setting of an Evensong canticle), "it is all up for grabs." I find that view too narrow; but another new form of clerical tyranny is equally unhelpful—not the tyranny of the rubrics, but the tyranny of the priest's liturgical views. In the name of the priest's concept of more relevant liturgy, what the assembly is given is sometimes the idiosyncrasies of an individual priest—ritual oddities reflecting what the presider or celebrant finds personally *meaningful*. This is simply a new form of clericalism.

The rubrics serve an important basic purpose during normal situations, enabling us to share a common experience: common prayer. The consequences of ignoring them, as has become rather common, can raise serious pastoral issues. I remember a Eucharist I attended at which the priest announced to us as he went along what was to come next. Since he was being "creative"—how sad that such a positive word can be connected to such a negative experience—each member of the congregation was obliged to have a kind of one-on-one experience with the presider. Contrary to the intent of good ritual, what unfolded did not draw us together into the unity that liturgy is called to nourish.

By coincidence, I had come that day from a hospital in which someone I loved very much was desperately ill. I earnestly wanted to share in the prayer of the Church and to find support in that from the community of faith. But the priest's "creativity" turned the Eucharist that day into an alienating experience. Rubrics, if properly engaged, do protect the congregation from the whims of the clergy. There is, of course, a need for creativity in the Church's liturgical prayer; without it, the liturgy can become dry and formalistic. But the creativity that is needed is not the idiosyncratic whim of the presider. Even in an "experimental rite," the participants need to share the experience as a community, not as isolated individuals wondering what will come next.[14]

So what is it that rubrics offer that, in a liturgical tradition such as ours, serves to build up our unity in the Body of Christ? Rubrics are not an end in themselves—they are not liturgical rules whose point is simply to be obeyed. The liturgy is the common prayer of the Church, and the purpose of the rubrics is to offer us the structure for a shared experience. Our common faith is nourished through that very commonality—familiar words and signs that strengthen our unity of faith through the proclamation of Scripture and the celebration of the sacramental rites. In a word, what a ritual does is not to enforce a monotonous repetition, but rather, by placing us on familiar ground, to remind us in our *anamnesis* of what God has done from Creation to this very day, and to invite us, as we "remember," to give thanks and praise, and expectantly to wait upon God who in Jesus has promised always to be with us.[15]

The role of the priest, whose privilege it is time and again to stand at the altar and to preside at this Meal, is to be there as a servant—a servant of

---

14. Cf. my "Liturgical Creativity," in Mark Searle, ed., *Parish: A Place for Worship* (Collegeville, MN: Liturgical Press, 1981), 81–96.

15. Matthew 28:20.

God's people. The eucharistic celebration is not all about the priest; in fact, the presider should "preside" and not dominate the ritual action. In that perspective, the rubrics serve as a kind of safeguard, to remind us all that this is the prayer of the whole Body of Christ.

CHAPTER 9

Liturgy
on Major Occasions

L ITURGICAL CELEBRATIONS ON SPECIAL
DAYS can raise particular questions. The
building blocks out of which such liturgies are shaped—the Liturgy of the Word and the
rites related to the proclamation of the Eucharistic
Prayer—are basic to any liturgical rite, no matter
how simple or how complex. The principal liturgy
on Sundays—the Eucharist as "the principal act of
Christian worship on the Lord's Day"[1]—includes all
the basic elements for any major liturgical event.

---

1. BCP, 13.

What a major occasion requires is the incorporation into that basic structure of the particular elements that are distinctive to the event. In other words, when a major liturgical celebration is to take place, those responsible for planning it do not begin from scratch: a great part of what is needed for such a liturgy is already in place.

This means that the distinctive elements need to be planned with great attention to detail, and with an eye to the often difficult task of determining how those elements will be appropriately blended into the structure. This planning and its implementation are critical considerations.

One common misunderstanding is the idea that an increased length of time required for the service conveys its importance. We do not make an event important by making it longer, by including more music than the ritual structure can bear, or by inserting elements that do not support the primary focus of the event itself. Length is not a guarantee of effective solemnity.

The problem of excessive length can result when the rites and the music are planned by two different groups. At the ordination of a bishop many years ago, an anthem was inserted at the point in the liturgy when the new bishop would be given the cope and miter. In the minds of the planners, this offered an opportunity for the choir of the parish where the new bishop had been rector to have a musical role in the ordination. The anthem chosen by the choir director was not known to the liturgical planners, and so the giving of the cope and miter, which took less than a minute, was "accompanied" by a ten-minute anthem while the congregation of almost a thousand people stood waiting for the seemingly interminable music to end. It seems too obvious to warrant a reminder that the various 'pieces' of a liturgy form a single whole—they are not merely items listed on a program.

The common purpose of all liturgical celebrations is to offer praise to God and to nourish the faith of the participants, not to exhaust them. Careful attention to detail becomes even more important in the planning of a "great occasion" rite. Church musicians are familiar with the phrase "pull out all the stops," and there are moments when the music supports a dramatic point in the celebration, but for that to occur in a constructive way, sensitive planning is essential.

I am not suggesting that all liturgies should be brief, although I must admit that Benedictine attitudes about the liturgy have been a major influence on my liturgical priorities, and the Benedictine sense in general is that "less is more." There is a profound truth in the power of understatement, especially when it comes to ritual events. The Franciscan liturgist William Cieslak once commented to me that "when the clergy and people have lost a sense of the meaning of a rite, they often insert supplementary elements to give it meaning," and it is such secondary elements which often draw the primary attention of the participants. The point is that the meaning of the rite is not something which is added on—it is integral to the rite itself, and to engage that meaning, we must enter into the ritual and its symbols deeply.

We need to learn that the purpose of the liturgy is not to entertain us, but rather to celebrate our common faith and to nourish it. This is our profound but simple task: to proclaim the Word of God and to celebrate what St. Augustine called "the Word made visible"—the sacraments. We need to be attentive so that additions do not obscure that primary purpose. There are liturgical rites which by their nature tend to be long, for example, the Holy Saturday Vigil, ordinations, or a major feast day. But there is an important difference between what might be called "organic length" and length that is the product of stringing a long series of items together.

Think of those liturgies on a major occasion, which perhaps have lasted two hours, or even, as at the Easter Vigil, for three hours. They often conclude leaving participants feeling energized, lifted up by the spiritual and personal nourishment that has been mediated through the common celebration. Length in itself is not the problem. I am convinced that "integral length" is experienced positively, but stands in sharp contrast to liturgies that seem to be made up of a series of unrelated parts.

Every liturgical act, whatever its length, requires structural balance. I am referring here to an integrity of structure that is fundamental in all the arts. The English art critic Clive Bell (1881–1964) spoke of this phenomenon as "significant form,"[2] and I think this speaks directly to the question of the quality of the liturgical act. It is not a matter of length or of a particular aesthetic norm in music or architecture, for example, by which each liturgical act would be tested. It is for me the awesome simplicity in which all the parts are joined in a convincing "whole." With regard to the liturgy, this can be found in a simple gathering of worshippers or it can be found in a great solemn liturgy into which every aesthetic resource available is incorporated.

The challenge here for laity and clergy who carry the responsibility of liturgical leadership in a particular community is to understand both the *craft* of liturgy and the nature of that particular community; unlike a dramatic performance, the liturgy is an act of faith, grounded in the life of a particular community. Inevitably each liturgical

---

2. Clive Bell, "The Aesthetic Hypothesis," in *Art* (New York: Capricorn Books, 1958), 15–34.

act has an aesthetic dimension, but it is more than that: the aesthetic dimension is the means by which the liturgical act engages our senses as well as our minds. The liturgy engages our full humanity: it is sensual. This aesthetic dimension of liturgy includes a number of aspects, with music perhaps first to come to mind. Music's role in creating and supporting the structural balance of a liturgical rite is fundamental. Some stories:

1. The opening procession at an ordination liturgy began, and after the initial exchange between the bishop and the ordinands, we arrived at the Liturgy of the Word. There were three readings: I noted that rather brief readings had been chosen, but there was nothing brief about the hymns placed between them. The hymns were long—the Scripture was short. Rather than serving to support the centrality of the Scriptures, the music chosen created "a hymn-sing with brief scenes from Scripture," as I later described it to one of the planners. The energy required for the singing of these long hymns eroded the attention which was owed to the hearing of the biblical readings.

   The role of music in the liturgy must be structurally integral: no matter how popular certain hymns may be, planners must weigh their selection alert to questions of balance: in a Liturgy of the Word, the experience should confirm to the hearers that the primary focus is in the proclamation of Scripture, and any hymns that are chosen must support that primary emphasis and not stand in rivalry to it.

2. It was the hundredth anniversary of a great parish: the bishop was present, as well as an extraordinary number of laity and clergy,, and the church was filled to the last pew. By any definition, it was a great occasion— one at which it is tempting to pull out all the stops. The bishop knocked at the door for the entrance at exactly 11:00 a.m. He sang "The Lord be with you" before the collect of that liturgy at 11:30 a.m. For the half-hour between, we were given, in effect, a superb concert of choral music, but the procession itself required scarcely ten minutes. So once the bishop reached the altar, the large congregation continued to stand for another twenty minutes while the choir performed very lengthy settings of the Ordinary. A Roman Catholic priest who was with me that day suddenly sat down; later I was able to ask him if he was ill. He replied, "No. I realized that the liturgy had become a concert—and I sit at a concert." Once the collect was over, the enormous congregation collapsed onto the pews and, I suspect, were too exhausted to listen to the

reading of Scripture. The imbalance eroded the solemnity of that great day.

Both of these examples are related to the issue of intelligent planning and attention to such details as timing. The great temptation for liturgical planners is to insert just one or two more items, for whatever reason, with the effect that balance is impaired and a great occasion becomes an exhausting one.

When important events in the life of the Church (or of a diocese or an individual parish) come along, these events require particular attention to the specific *quality* of such an occasion. By their nature, they are *celebrative*—but this does not mean that they must be double the length of a normal liturgy. This requires a coordinated attention on the part of the planners to *all aspects of the rite*, so that there is an integration of all the diverse parts of the rite into an experience of the whole. For this to happen, the planners must accept the difficult discipline of saying "no" to elements that will, even with the best of intentions, undermine that experience.

CHAPTER 10

A Final Word

WHY DOES ANY OF THIS matter? Do questions about ritual merit specialized attention—the type of scrutiny we have offered in this book? It has been suggested that liturgists are concerned about "smells and bells"—about trivial details concerning the liturgy. Those of us who teach liturgical studies know quite well that in some contexts, an excess of concern has been given to liturgical minutia. But if my primary concern in this book has been clear, I hope the reader has seen that a serious commitment to liturgical prayer is not obsessed about the length of a surplice.

Having said that, I do have an opinion about a

great many matters that might be labeled 'liturgical trivia.' Most of the people who teach in this field have opinions—often very strong opinions, but our primary purpose is the service of the people of God, the building up of the Body of Christ. What we teach is rooted in what we have learned and what we have experienced in our own lives of faith. It was to my great benefit that my teachers, recognized experts in the study of the liturgy, were first of all people of profound faith and commitment. What they taught me about liturgy and sacramental theology planted in me a very strong sense of priorities. My goal here has been to share that sense.

If one word were to characterize my goal in liturgical performance, it would be "restraint." But there again we see that so easily misunderstood word: *performance.* As we noted early in this book, it can be a misleading word when it is applied to the liturgy. Our normal association with the term is linked to a theatrical or musical performance. And there can be no doubt that at times, some who have been given liturgical responsibilities have understood *liturgical performance* in that misleading sense. I have often heard reference to "the drama of the liturgy." We need to be very cautious about such language because it can convey a certain sense (perhaps unintended) of artificiality as in "to put on a show." Liturgy is performative because it embodies a sacramental intention as an outward sign of an interior grace.

I still remember a program for parish priests and their musicians. As a whole, it was a fruitful conference, but one day a member of the group asked me if I would "put on a High Mass for us while we are here." Thinking that he would understand, I responded, "But there is no major feast day this week." And he said, "What difference does that make?" It seemed that for him, liturgical performance meant something quite different from what I understood it to be.

What we *do* in a particular liturgy must come from within—not some decorative element that we apply from the outside. The heart of authentic liturgy is always the inner reality of faith embodied, using fragile human forms that are our stewardship of the gifts of grace. It is in this sense that we may speak of the liturgy as 'performative.' The act *does* what it *says*. Too great a preoccupation with ritual details can erode the inner integrity of the rite as sacramental act and, in the experience of the people gathered, can put the primary emphasis in the wrong place.

The liturgical act is, in its essence, a very simple thing. In a book that was perhaps the most influential liturgical study published in the entire twentieth century, the Anglican Benedictine Dom Gregory Dix wrote movingly of this insight:

> At the heart of it all is the eucharistic
> action, a thing of an absolute simplicity—
> the taking, blessing, breaking and giving
> of bread and the taking, blessing and
> giving of a cup of wine and water, as
> these were first done with their new
> meaning by a young Jew before and
> after supper with His friends on the
> night before He died. . . . He had told
> his friends to do this henceforward with
> the new meaning "for the *anamnesis*" of
> Him, and they have done it always since.[1]

On the part of the presider at the Eucharist, this is achieved not by ignoring details, but by being so attentive to details that the "absolute simplicity" of what is being done comes through and the people are not distracted by confusing manual actions and trivial gestures. This means that for presiders, and for those who prepare future presiders, one must ask some fundamental questions about the gestures that are chosen to be done, or not to be done:

- Why am I doing this?
- How did it originate?
- What does it mean to me?
- What does it say to the members of the congregation who observe this gesture?

---

1. Gregory Dix, *The Shape of the Liturgy* (Westminster: Dacre Press, 1945), 743–44.

We no longer understand the Eucharist as a quasi-private devotion of the priest which laity are permitted to observe. By the grace of God, we have recovered the sense that it is an action which is *celebrated* by the entire assembly under the pastoral leadership of the ordained priest. What the presider *does* at the altar can either separate the people as observers or it can invite them to share as full participants.

In the past, some of those who have greatly valued the liturgy in the life of the Church and understood it as central to the life of faith, have unintentionally contributed to the erosion of its role in Christian faith and practice by being more concerned with its beauty and perfection than with its power as a primary source of union in God. In this sense, the liturgy is not so much to be admired as to be a source of grace in our journey to God. Our fragile and fallible humanity is transformed by God's grace and finds its most profound fulfillment in praise.

Christians have over many centuries witnessed to the fact that in our gathering with those who share a faith in Christ Jesus—gathered to obey what our Lord commanded us to do—we find him present. In the words of the Puritan divine John

Cotton (1585–1652), we are "drenched in grace."[2] My hope here has been to challenge all who have read this book to enter ever more deeply into these sacramental acts in which the *mirabilia Dei*—the wonderful works of God—embrace us as God's own people and remind us of the glory that is to be revealed.

---

2. John Cotton, *Way of Life, or God's Way and Course: The Pouring Out of the Spirit* (London: Printed by M.F. for L. Fawne and S. Gellibrand, 1641), 105–06.